Cognition and Reality

A Series of Books in Psychology

Editors:
Richard C. Atkinson
Jonathan Freedman
Gardner Lindzey
Richard F. Thompson

Cognition and Reality

PRINCIPLES AND IMPLICATIONS OF COGNITIVE PSYCHOLOGY

ULRIC NEISSER

Cornell University

W. H. FREEMAN AND COMPANY
New York

Library of Congress Cataloging in Publication Data

Neisser, Ulric.
  Cognition and reality.

  Bibliography: p.
  Includes indexes.
  1. Cognition. I. Title.
BF311.N43   153.4   76-24813
ISBN 0-7167-0478-1
ISBN 0-7167-0477-3 pbk.

Printed in the United States of America

11 12 13 14   VB   4 3 2 1 0 8 9

For James J. Gibson and Eleanor J. Gibson,
in gratitude for insight, argument, and friendship

Contents

Preface

This book is an attempt to deal with several questions that have seemed increasingly important since my earlier survey of cognitive psychology appeared in 1967. The first concerns the conception of human nature that is, or ought to be, implicit in the idea of cognition. It seemed clear from the beginning that this conception was different from that offered by other approaches to psychology, but the implications of the differences have never been spelled out. Perhaps as a result, the actual development of cognitive psychology in the last few years has been disappointingly narrow, focusing inward on the analysis of specific experimental situations rather than outward toward the world beyond the laboratory. The second question is more specifically concerned with this development: what is happening in contemporary cognitive psychology, and what are we to think of it? There is no disputing the ingenuity and sophistication of much current research, but there is at least some reason to wonder whether its overall direction is genuinely productive.

The third question began independently of the others, but became interwoven with them in the course of my concern with it. In recent years, James J. Gibson has mounted an important challenge to the assumptions on which most of today's cognitive psychology is based. Gibson is my good friend and valued colleague; I have been unable to avoid taking his challenge seriously. His arguments have made me realize that the notion of *information processing* deserves a closer examination. In particular, the amount and kind of processing that a stimulus is assumed to undergo necessarily depends on related assumptions about the nature of that stimulus; that is, on how the theorist chooses to describe it. (I am particularly grateful to James Farber for fruitful discussions of this issue.) Nevertheless, although I am sufficiently indebted to James and Eleanor Gibson to have dedicated this book to them, my argument is not really compatible with "Gibsonian" principles. To their dismay, I have found it necessary to suppose that the perceiver has certain cognitive structures, called *schemata*, that function to pick up the information that the environment offers. This notion is central in my attempt to reconcile the concepts of information processing and information pickup, both of which capture too much of the truth to be ignored. In addition, it offers a connecting link between perception and the higher mental processes.

The last of the questions that generated this book concerns the conceptions of attention, capacity, and consciousness. In writing *Cognitive Psychology* a decade ago, I deliberately avoided theorizing about consciousness. It seemed to me that psychology was not ready to tackle the issue, and that any attempt to do so would lead only to philosophically naive and fumbling speculation. Unfortunately, these fears have been realized; many current models of cognition treat consciousness as if it were just a particular stage of processing in a mechanical flow of information. Because I am sure that these models are wrong, it has seemed important to develop an alternative interpretation of the data on which they are based. The reader should be warned that Chapter 5, in which these issues are discussed, presents a personal and unorthodox account of attention phenomena rather than a generally accepted view.

So many people have read fragments and drafts of these chapters that it is impossible to thank them all individually for their help. I do want to acknowledge the particularly valuable criticism of J. J. Gibson, Herbert Pick, Jack Catlin, Elizabeth Spelke, and especially Arden Neisser. I have also benefited from the continuous flow of ideas and experiments generated by a very talented group of graduate students who have been working on attention and related issues with me in the last two years: Elizabeth Spelke, William Hirst, Robert Becklen, David Littman, Richard Evans, and Maurice Haltom.

The initial drafts of some of these chapters were written while I was a Fellow at the Center for Advanced Study in the Behavioral Sciences during 1973 and 1974, and I am grateful for the Center's support. My editor, W. Hayward Rogers of W. H. Freeman and Company, has been more than understanding during the one and a half years of further struggle and procrastination since my return to Cornell, and my colleagues in the psychology department have been both good-natured and helpful. Roberta Wallenbeck typed innumerable drafts with cheerful accuracy, and Carol Koken prepared the final manuscript with remarkable speed and skill.

Cognition and Reality

Introduction

Cognition is the activity of knowing: the acquisition, organization, and use of knowledge. It is something that organisms do and in particular something that people do. For this reason the study of cognition is a part of psychology, and theories of cognition are psychological theories.

At one time, this relationship was so obvious that it required no comment. When psychology emerged as a separate discipline a hundred years ago, it was extensively concerned with such matters as sensation, perception, association, imagery, and attention. The principal goal of psychological science was the analysis of "mental processes," which usually meant cognitive processes. Unfortunately, the chief method used for this analysis was a special form of introspection, in which highly trained observers reported on the activities of their own conscious minds. In the long run, this method proved unsatisfactory. By the 1930s it had fallen into disrepute; introspection was abandoned (at least in America), and the focus of psychological work had moved to motivation, emotion, and action.

Textbooks of the history of psychology usually attribute the downfall of this early approach to the inadequacy of its basic procedure. Introspection is a sloppy tool, yielding results that may be biased by the act of observation itself. Different observers may give divergent introspective accounts of the "same" process, and there is no way to resolve their disagreements. That is true enough, as far as it goes, but another reason deserves consideration as well. Because psychology is about people, it cannot shirk the responsibility of dealing with fundamental questions about human nature. In general, its audience already holds certain views on these questions. Every age has its own conceptions—men are free or determined, rational or irrational; they can discover the truth or they are doomed to illusion. In the long run, psychology must treat these issues or be found wanting. A seminal psychological theory can change the beliefs of a whole society, as psychoanalysis, for example, has surely done. This can only happen, however, if the theory has something to say about what people do in real, culturally significant situations. What it says must not be trivial, and it must make some kind of sense to the participants in these situations themselves. If a theory lacks these qualities—if it does not have what is nowadays called "ecological validity"—it will be abandoned sooner or later.

The conception of human nature held by the classical introspective psychologists was inadequate in just this way. Narrow, overly rational, applicable only to laboratory situations, it lacked any clear account of how people interact with the world. Human beings become what they are by growing up in a particular culture and a particular environment, but the introspectionists had no theory of cognitive development. People are driven by motives that they do not understand and shaped by experiences they cannot remember, but there was no theory of unconscious processes. People act on what they know and are changed by the consequences of their actions, but there was no serious theory of behavior. Even perception and memory were interpreted in ways that made little contact with everyday experience. In short, introspective psychology left out nearly everything that ordinary people thought important. It is not surprising, then, that it was abandoned in favor of more promising ideas.

Two of the approaches that succeeded it are still very much with us: psychoanalysis and behaviorism. They have succeeded where introspective psychology failed. This is not only because they have offered valid insights about human nature—although neither would have survived without some grain of truth—but because they are, or claim to be, applicable to ordinary life. Theory and application enrich each other. A clinical or experimental finding throws new light on some class of events in the everyday world, and observations made in that world suggest new hypotheses. Indeed, explicit striving for "relevance" has characterized both approaches from the first. The founders of these schools, Freud and Watson, were keenly aware that their work had implications beyond the consulting room and the laboratory. Both set out deliberately to change the prevailing conception of human nature. Freud tried to convince the world that the urges of the libido were the paramount sources of human motives and that conscious activity occupied only the smallest and least powerful part of the mind. He succeeded to a remarkable extent, as nearly every cultural institution from the art gallery to the law court can bear witness. Watson and his successor Skinner maintained that people are almost infinitely malleable, and that the consequences of human behavior are crucially important while the mental activity that accompanies the behavior is not. These claims are also being widely accepted, judging by the increasing use of behavior modification and behavior therapy in many contexts and by the growing fear that behavioral science will soon be used to manipulate people on a large scale.

A purist might maintain that the reaction of the general public is entirely irrelevant to scientific psychology. I think he would be wrong. Public interest is no indication of a theory's validity, but it suggests that the theory may be saying something important. A psychology that cannot interpret ordinary experience is ignoring almost the whole range of its natural subject matter. It may hope to emerge from the laboratory some day with a new array of important ideas, but that outcome is unlikely unless it is already working with principles whose applicability to natural situations can be foreseen.

From the First World War to the 1960s, behaviorism and psychoanalysis (or their offshoots) so dominated American psychology that cognitive processes were almost entirely ignored. Not many psychologists were interested in the question of how knowledge is acquired. Perception, the most fundamental cognitive act, was studied primarily by a small group following the "Gestalt" tradition and a few other psychologists who worked on the measurement and physiology of sensory processes. Piaget and his collaborators studied cognitive development, but their contributions received little recognition. There was no work on attention. Research on memory was never entirely abandoned, but it dealt primarily with the learning of "nonsense syllables," in tightly defined laboratory procedures of little generality. As a result, the public image of psychology was that it dealt chiefly with sex, adjustment, and behavioral control.

This situation has changed radically in the last few years. Mental processes have again become a lively focus of interest. A new field called *cognitive psychology* has come into being. It studies perception, memory, attention, pattern recognition, problem solving, the psychology of language, cognitive development, and a host of other problems that had lain dormant for half a century. Technical journals once top heavy with articles on animal behavior are now filled with reports of cognitive experiments, and new journals are mushrooming: *Cognitive Psychology, Cognition, Memory and Cognition, Perception and Psychophysics*. Grants for cognitive research are easily obtained, and nearly every major university has a cognitive laboratory. Piaget's work has been rediscovered and hailed.

There were several reasons for this turn of events, but the most important was probably the advent of the computer. This was not just because computers allow one to conduct experiments more easily or analyze data more thoroughly, though they do. Rather, it was because the activities of the computer itself seemed in some ways akin to cognitive processes. Computers accept information, manipulate symbols, store items in "memory" and retrieve them again, classify inputs, recognize patterns, and so on. Whether they do these things just like people

was less important than that they do them at all. The
coming of the computer provided a much-needed reas-
surance that cognitive processes were real; that they
could be studied and perhaps understood. It also provided a new vocabulary and a new set of concepts for
dealing with cognition; terms like *information, input,
processing, coding,* and *subroutine* soon became commonplace. Some theorists even maintained that all psychological theories should be explicitly written in the
form of computer programs.[1] Others differed, and continue to differ,[2] but no one doubts the importance of the
computer metaphor for contemporary psychology.

As the concept of information processing developed,
the attempt to trace the flow of information through the
"system" (i.e., the mind) became a paramount goal of
the new field. (I stated this goal explicitly myself, in a
book called *Cognitive Psychology.*[3]) The rapid development of several new experimental techniques,
devised by Broadbent, Sperling, Sternberg, and others,
created an exhilarating sense of progress. These techniques were only the beginning; there has been a vir-
tual deluge of new procedures, most of which rely on
precise timing of stimuli or responses while avoiding
the necessity of introspection altogether. The proliferation of these ingenious and scientifically respectable
methods seemed at first—and still seems to many—a
sign that the new cognitive psychology would succeed
in avoiding whatever pitfall had claimed the old.

Such optimism may have been premature. The study
of information processing has momentum and prestige,
but it has not yet committed itself to any conception of
human nature that could apply beyond the confines of
the laboratory. And within that laboratory, its basic assumptions go little further than the computer model to

which it owes its existence. There is still no account of how people act in or interact with the ordinary world. Indeed, the assumptions that underlie most contemporary work on information processing are surprisingly like those of nineteenth-century introspective psychology, though without introspection itself.

If cognitive psychology commits itself too thoroughly to this model, there may be trouble ahead. Lacking in ecological validity, indifferent to culture, even missing some of the main features of perception and memory as they occur in ordinary life, such a psychology could become a narrow and uninteresting specialized field. There are already indications that this may be happening. The proliferation of new techniques is no longer encouraging; it has become oppressive. In a recent article Allan Newell tabulates no fewer than 59 experimental paradigms of current interest.[4] He wonders explicitly whether another generation of such work, and the development of still more techniques, will make us any wiser. Fifty-seven of the paradigms on Newell's list are based on artificial laboratory situations; the only ones with even a shred of ecological validity are playing chess and looking at the moon.

This trend can only be reversed, I think, if the study of cognition takes a more "realistic" turn, in several senses of that word. First, cognitive psychologists must make a greater effort to understand cognition as it occurs in the ordinary environment and in the context of natural purposeful activity. This would not mean an end to laboratory experiments, but a commitment to the study of variables that are ecologically important rather than those that are easily manageable. Second, it will be necessary to pay more attention to the details of the real world in which perceivers and thinkers live, and the fine structure of information which that world makes available to them. We may have been lavishing too much effort on hypothetical models of the mind and not enough on analyzing the environment that the mind has been shaped to meet. Third, psychology must somehow come to terms with the sophistication and complexity of the cognitive skills that people are really capable of acquiring, and with the fact that these skills undergo systematic development. A satisfactory theory of human cognition can hardly be established by experiments that provide inexperienced subjects with brief opportunities to perform novel and meaningless tasks. Finally, cognitive psychologists must examine the implications of their work for more fundamental questions: human nature is too important to be left to the behaviorists and psychoanalysts.

The aim of this book is to show that such an enterprise is possible. Indeed, it is already under way; there are many flourishing lines of research on which it can be based. The developmental studies of Piaget and T. G. R. Bower, the perceptual work of James J. and Eleanor J. Gibson, the renewed interest in natural cognitive maps, the shift to semantic theories of language and to naturalistic observation of language acquisition—these and many other developments can be seen as contributions to a meaningful cognitive psychology. I will rely heavily on them in the argument that follows. In places where no such underpinnings are yet available, it has been necessary to fill in the gaps with speculation and hypothesis. Even if some of my speculations turn out to be wrong, they may encourage others to offer more adequate hypotheses of their own.

Although my aim is to treat all aspects of cognition in a realistic framework, much of the argument in the following pages is specifically concerned with perception. In part, this is because perceiving is the basic cognitive activity out of which all others must emerge; the later chapters (especially Chapters 7 and 8) show how this may happen for imagination and language. Even more important, however, is that perception is where cognition and reality meet. I do not think the nature of that encounter is well understood by most psychologists. The prevailing view of it tends to glorify the perceiver, who is said to process, transform, recode, assimilate, or generally give shape to what would otherwise be a meaningless chaos. This cannot be right; perception, like evolution, is surely a matter of discovering what the environment is really like and adapting to it.

Reacting sharply against the information-processing view, James J. Gibson[5] has proposed a theory of perception in which mental events play no role at all; the perceiver directly picks up the information that the world offers him. The conceptual scheme that Gibson has developed around this theory is a valuable one, and I will make extensive use of it here. Nevertheless, the Gibsonian view of perception also seems inadequate, if only because it says so little about the perceiver's contribution to the perceptual act. There must be definite kinds of structure in every perceiving organism to enable it to notice certain aspects of the environment rather than others, or indeed to notice anything at all.

The first part of the book is concerned with the resolution of this paradox. It can be resolved by treating perception as an activity that takes place over time— time during which the anticipatory schemata of the perceiver can come to terms with the information offered by his environment. Chapter 2 deals specifically with contemporary theories of perception and their relationships to the hypothesis proposed here. Chapter 3 examines the nature of visual perception in everyday life, stressing the difference between ordinary seeing on the one hand and the restricted conditions of most perceptual experiments on the other. The argument comes to a head in Chapter 4, which tries to offer specific definitions of *schema, information pickup,* and other central concepts. The same chapter shows how the present notion of schema can be used to interpret the development of perception in infancy, and can accommodate our perception of the meaningful as well as the merely geographical aspects of objects and events.

Chapter 5 is essentially a long digression on the concepts of attention, capacity, and consciousness. By the time he has reached it, the reader will have discovered that my argument has a negative as well as a positive side: in advocating one kind of cognitive psychology, I cannot avoid criticizing the assumptions of another. The villains of the piece are the mechanistic information-processing models, which treat the mind as a fixed-capacity device for converting discrete and meaningless inputs into conscious percepts. Because recent experimental studies of attention appear to support these models, it seemed necessary to suggest another interpretation of their results. The discussion of attention also stresses the importance of studying skilled achievement rather than initial performance in cognitive tasks and the dangers of using casual introspection as the basis for mechanistic hypotheses.

In Chapter 6 the perceiver, who remained more or less at rest in the first half of the book, is set free to move around in his environment. This immediately provides him with significant new kinds of information, as well as with a more extensive cognitive structure to take account of them. The relation between this *cognitive map* and the schemata embedded within it is taken as a model for the organization of complex processes in general. As it happens, cognitive maps can be used in more than one way: although their essential function is to guide us in our travels, it has been known since ancient times that they can also serve as effective mnemonic devices. In this capacity, of course, a cognitive map is a particular sort of mental image. Chapter 7 takes up the question of mental imagery directly. It suggests that images are essentially perceptual anticipations, preparations for picking up certain kinds of information. The hypothesis is supported by a review of modern experiments on imagery.

Chapter 8, perhaps the most speculative in the book, deals with speech and language. It is particularly concerned with the *introspective* use of language, i.e., with what happens as a person describes the mental images considered in the chapter before. Since this question cannot be resolved unless certain basic issues concerning the nature and acquisition of speech have been clarified first, an attempt is made to do so.

The final chapter addresses more general questions. Perception and cognition are usually not just operations in the head, but transactions with the world. These transactions do not merely *in*form the perceiver, they also *trans*form him. Each of us is created by the cognitive acts in which he engages. This fact, which the earlier parts of the book try to document and clarify, has significant implications for the frequently suggested possibility that psychologists might use their specialized knowledge to predict or control human behavior in its social context. The nature of cognition seems to make such predictability unattainable in principle as well as in practice. If it is, other branches of psychology besides the study of cognition may have to aim at more realistic goals.

Notes

1. Newell, Shaw, and Simon (1958); Newell and Simon (1972); Anderson and Bower (1973); Winston (1975).
2. Most of the resistance to computer modeling is passive; psychologists simply continue to make theories of other kinds. A few theorists have been bold enough to suggest explicit limits on what can be programmed (Dreyfus, 1972; Gunderson, 1971). I set out my own views on the limitations of contemporary "artificial intelligence" some time ago (Neisser, 1963), and have recently brought them up to date (Neisser, 1976).
3. Neisser (1967).
4. Newell (1973).
5. Gibson (1966, 1976).

Theories of
Perception

It seems obvious that we have to obtain knowledge before we can use it. Books on cognitive psychology usually deal with perceiving before they consider remembering and other "higher" processes, probably for this reason. Matters are not really so simple, however. Perception itself depends on the skill and experience of the perceiver—on what he knows in advance. You will not pick up much information from this book, for example, unless you can already read the language in which it is written. More subtly, what you see in my argument will depend not only on what I may say but also on what you know (and believe) before you start. The same principle applies to briefer experiences: What you learn from the second half of this very sentence will depend on what you have already picked up from the first.

This relation between the present and the past does not mean that you must remember the first half of a

sentence by the time you get around to perceiving the
second half, as if two distinctly different mental processes were being combined. The fact is simply that the
act of reading takes time. It does not occur in a moment.
The information on the printed page becomes available
to the reader only over time, and reading must be organized over time as well. In this book, I will argue that
all ordinary perceiving has just these characteristics.

Not only reading but also listening, feeling, and looking are skillful activities that occur over time. All of
them depend upon preexisting structures, here called
schemata, which direct perceptual activity and are
modified as it occurs. Perceiving does not require remembering in the ordinary sense, but it is an activity in
which both the immediate past and the remote past are
brought to bear upon the present. Genuine remembering (recall of past experiences) is also such an activity,
of course, as are imagining, speaking, thinking, and
every other form of cognition. I hope to show that all of
them are best understood as applications of the same
fundamental cognitive structures.

The cumulative, internally guided nature of perception has not often been discussed by psychologists. This
may be because nearly all treatments of the topic are
based on vision. They come only later, if at all, to senses
like hearing and touch in which the role of temporal
structure is more obvious.[1] From an evolutionary point
of view, this sequence is a strange one. Phylogeneti-
cally, touching is older than looking or listening. Even
very primitive animals feel objects and explore surfaces
with parts of their bodies, acquiring information over
time by doing so; only the more recently evolved
species can see and hear. Nevertheless, active touch
has been little studied, while vision and hearing each

have what amounts to their own scientific establishment. Some reasons for this state of affairs will be considered later.

For whatever reason, then, most theories of perception have been constructed with vision in mind. Moreover, their model has not been the active looking of everyday life, but rather the restricted gaze of a subject who holds his head and eyes as still as possible or else is presented with a flash of illumination so brief that he has no time to move them. These precautions are routinely taken to ensure that the subject gets only a static and uncomplicated *retinal image*. Theories of how such an image might be interpreted or processed have served as paradigms for perceptual theory in general. We will briefly review the "modal model" that this approach has produced, and then consider alternative possibilities.

Visual perception as information processing

Descartes may have been the first person to actually see a retinal image. He dissected out the eye of a bull, aimed it at a real scene, and examined the inverted image of the scene that was projected on the back of the excised eye.[2] It has often been tempting to suppose that ordinary perceiving is essentially the same process: that somehow people actually see their own retinal images, and thus are indirectly informed about the scene before them. Yet this cannot be true, and the attempt to theorize as if it were true has led to much confusion. If there were an "inner man" who looked at the retinal image from inside the head, his perceptual processes would require just as much explanation as those of the whole man. Indeed, such a homunculus would have quite a few problems of his own. The image that he supposedly looks at is upside-down, foreshortened, and the wrong size; it exists in two slightly discrepant versions, and it changes constantly as the eyes move. Many sophisticated theories have been advanced to explain how he might solve these problems, but real perceivers do not have them. We do not see our retinal images; we see the real environment of objects and events (and ourselves). Of course, we see it by picking up information available in the light,[3] but this is an activity extended in time. It need not be organized in terms of momentary retinal "snapshots" at all, and the similarity or dissimilarity between perceived objects and their projected images is irrelevant to it.

The philosophical problems created by the notion of seeing the retinal image have long been recognized, and no modern psychologist holds exactly this view. Although many contemporary theorists still begin their accounts of vision with the same image, they have a different hypothesis about how it is used. According to modern doctrine, the image is not looked at but *processed*. Certain specific mechanisms in the visual system, called *detectors,* are assumed to initiate neural messages in response to certain equally specific features of the image. Information about these features is then passed on to higher stages of the brain. At the higher stages it is collated and combined with previously stored information in a series of processes that eventually results in perceptual experience. Theories of this type—internal information-processing theories—are often illustrated with flow charts. One such chart is given in Figure 1.

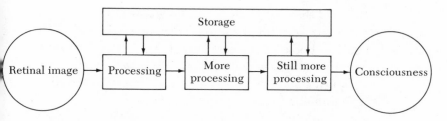

FIGURE 1. *The internal information-processing model of perception.*

A good deal of psychological and physiological evidence supports this general approach. Neural systems that respond selectively to orientations, curves, colors, and movements have been identified by electrophysiological methods. Moreover, certain illusions, adaptation effects, and patterns of reaction-time can be readily interpreted in terms of the activity of these detectors,[4] so the information that they pass on to higher centers is surely significant. It appears, however, that other aspects of perception are more difficult for such models to explain. Particular problems arise in connection with selection, unit formation, meaning, coherence, veridicality, and perceptual development. How does it happen that different people notice different aspects of the same real situation? Why are some portions of the retinal input treated as belonging to the same object, others as independent? Why do we often seem to perceive the meanings of events rather than their detectable surface features? How are successive glances at the same scene "integrated"? Why is perceiving almost always accurate, given the previously noted inadequacies of the retinal image? How is it that babies perceive *objects* from the very first, as they apparently do (see Chapter 4)? What happens in perceptual learning?

Some of these objections can be answered by modifications of the internal information-processing view. In an earlier book,[5] I suggested that the internal flow of perception involves two consecutive stages. In the first *preattentive* stage, features are detected and analyzed. This automatic process is usually followed by an act of construction, in which the perceiver "makes" one perceptual object rather than another. Since I have described the advantages of this view before, I will focus here on one of its difficulties. It fails to explain the veridicality of perception. If percepts are constructed, why are they usually accurate? Surely perceiving is not just a lucky way of having mental images![6] The answer must lie in the kind and quality of optical information available to the perceiver. The information must be specific enough in most cases to ensure that the constructed percept is true to the real object. But if this is admitted, the notion of "construction" seems almost superfluous. One is tempted to dispense with it altogether, as J. J. Gibson has done.[7]

The information in the light

Gibson's theory of perception does not begin with the retinal image. It starts with the pattern of ambient light, reflected from objects, that is available to be sampled at any given point in space. The complex structural properties of this *optic array* are determined by the actual nature and position of the objects. This structure *specifies* those objects; the information about them is in the light. When the observer or an object moves, certain higher-order characteristics of the optic array remain invariant while others change, and these invariants over time specify the layout of the environment still more precisely. The observer perceives simply by "picking up" these invariances. He may have to search for information but he need not process it, because it is all in the light already.

Gibson's view has certain striking advantages over the traditional one. The organism is not thought of as buffeted about by stimuli, but rather as attuned to properties of its environment that are objectively present, accurately specified, and veridically perceived. The emphasis on the pickup of information over time makes the theory applicable to haptic (touch-relevant) and acoustic information as well as to light, at least in principle. The most important thrust of the theory is to suggest that students of perception should develop new and richer descriptions of the stimulus information, rather than ever-subtler hypotheses about mental mechanisms. Gibson's "ecological optics" is one attempt at such a description. (I believe that recent descriptions of the optic array as a collection of spatial frequencies[8] represent another promising attempt, though Gibson himself has doubts about them.)

Despite these strengths, the theory remains unsatisfying in certain respects. Most obviously, it says nothing about what is in the perceiver's head. What kinds of cognitive structure does perception require? How do perceivers differ from one another? What happens when we choose what to see or how do we learn to see better? How are illusion and error possible if perception is simply the pickup of information that is already available and specific? How are we to conceive other cognitive processes—imagery, memory, thought— where the coupling between the organism and the environment is weak or nonexistent?

Some of these issues, especially those about cognitive development and perceptual learning, are met in the complementary work of Eleanor J. Gibson.[9] As she has shown, the difference between a skilled and an unskilled perceiver is not that the former adds anything to the stimulus but that he is able to gain more information from it: he detects features and higher-order structure to which the naive viewer is not sensitive. A newborn infant ignores information that older children and adults acquire effortlessly. For both of the Gibsons, the task of psychology is to describe this information. Yet that does not seem enough; another part of the job is to understand the cognitive structures internal to the perceiver and the manner in which they change.

The perceptual cycle

In my view, the cognitive structures crucial for vision are the anticipatory schemata that prepare the perceiver to accept certain kinds of information rather than others and thus control the activity of looking. Because we can see only what we know how to look for, it is these schemata (together with the information actually available) that determine what will be perceived. Perception is indeed a constructive process, but what is constructed is not a mental image appearing in consciousness where it is admired by an inner man. At each moment the perceiver is constructing anticipations of certain kinds of information, that enable him to accept it as it becomes available. Often he must actively explore the optic array to make it available, by moving his eyes or his head or his body. These explorations are directed by the anticipatory schemata, which are plans for per-

ceptual action as well as readinesses for particular kinds
of optical structure. The outcome of the explorations—
the information picked up—modifies the original
schema. Thus modified, it directs further exploration
and becomes ready for more information. This cycle is
diagrammed in Figure 2.

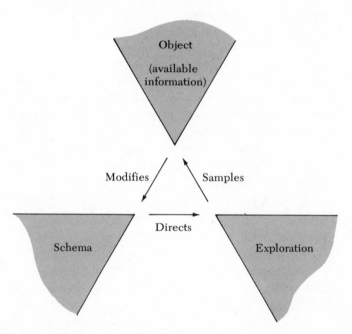

FIGURE 2. *The perceptual cycle.*

The information picked up in vision is necessarily
optical, consisting of patterns in the light over space and
time. But optical information can specify objects and
events at various levels of abstraction and meaning, and
a schema organized on one level need not be sensitive
to the others. If we happen to see someone smile, for
example, there may be information to specify (a) the

shapes of his teeth; (b) the changing positions of his lips; (c) the fact that he is carrying out a certain culturally-significant act; i.e., smiling; (d) something about his mood, which may be cheerful or sardonic or merely polite depending on the context in which the smile occurs. When we perceive his mood, we are not engaged in the same perceptual cycle as when we are attending to his lip movements. We develop a different (though perhaps overlapping) set of anticipations; we pick up information that extends over a different span of time; we do not use the information for the same purposes, and we will remember the event differently as a result. In this way, the concept of a perceptual cycle explains how one can perceive meaning as well as spatial position and form.

The schema assures the continuity of perception over time in two different ways. Because schemata are anticipations, they are the medium by which the past affects the future; information already acquired determines what will be picked up next. (This is the underlying mechanism of *memory*, though that term is best restricted to cases in which time and a change of situation intervene between the formation of the schema and its use.) In addition, however, some schemata are temporal in their very nature. When an object moves, for example, continuous and complex changes take place in the optic array. If it moves directly toward a perceiver, the optical projections of every bit of texture on its surface move outward; the pattern on the perceiver's retina undergoes a continuous expansion. We need not suppose that this expansion is picked up as a series of discrete and individually anticipated frames, although it can be simulated by such a series in a motion picture. The schema is attuned to the optical event as a whole. One can anticipate temporal patterns as well as spatial ones. This characteristic of schemata is even more obvious in the case of other sense modalities, as we will see shortly.

In choosing the model of Figure 2 over that of Figure 1, I do not mean to deny the existence of internal cognitive processes. It should be clear that the triangle labeled *schema* is highly structured. But this structure should not be conceived as a simple flow from the periphery to the mind; it subserves a continuously interactive process. I suspect that its parts are better conceived as embedded schemata that interact with their environment in their own right (see Figure 3, Chapter 6) than as discrete stages with input and output. Moreover, although the schema plays a critical role in every perceptual act, it is not a "percept," nor does it produce one anywhere in the perceiver's head. The act of perceiving does not terminate in a percept at all.[10] The schema is just one phase of an ongoing activity which relates the perceiver to his environment. The term *perception* applies properly to the entire cycle and not to any detached part of it. To be sure, schemata can be detached from the cycles in which they are originally embedded; such detachment is the basis of all the higher mental processes. What happens then is not perceiving, however, but imagining, planning, or intending.

This does not mean that we cannot pick up unanticipated information. Normally, however, the function of an unexpected stimulus is to initiate the cycle of perception proper; there is usually enough continuing information to support the cycle once it has begun. Even when there is not, the very act of searching for such information embeds what was picked up in some de-

gree of context. When this fails to happen—when a
stimulus is neither anticipated nor followed up by perceptual activity—it will have only limited and transient
effects on us.

The account of perception being proposed here[11] is
not intended as a radical alternative to the classical
theories but as a way to render them coherent with one
another and with everyday reality. The Gibsons are
surely right in their claim that the optic array (at a moving point of observation) provides accurate information
about the environment, which the perceiver picks up.
How could this be false? Those who treat perception as
information processing are also right: complex
mechanisms in the brain are involved in accepting this
information. So, too, is a third group of theorists, including Bruner and Gregory,[12] who have described perception as the testing and confirming of hypotheses. Each
of these views has focused on a single aspect of what is
normally a continuous and cyclic activity.

Haptic perception

It was noted earlier that the sense of touch has received much less scientific attention than vision or
hearing. Special journals are devoted to optics and to
acoustics, to research in vision and to disorders of hearing; entire laboratories specialize in psychoacoustics or
in visual research; Nobel Prizes have been awarded for
the discovery of basic mechanisms in both modalities.
Touch has far less glamor and prestige, and we know
correspondingly less about it.[13]

There are several reasons for this. Most obviously,
vision and hearing each have their own specialized
sense organs, mechanisms presenting tangible (!) chal-

lenges to the investigator. "How does the eye work?" and "How does the ear work?" sound like potentially answerable questions, and indeed they have turned out to be. Touch, the haptic sense, seems to have no specific machinery at all. The flow of haptic information in the nervous system is not funneled through any single structure analogous to the retina or to the basilar membrane. When you run your fingers over an object in the dark to determine its shape, you change the neural activity in receptor cells all the way from the skin of your fingertips to the joint of your elbow, and beyond. There is no place for an internal flow chart like Figure 1 to begin, and therefore no obvious place for research to begin either.

It is equally difficult to isolate or define the "stimulus" for touch. Nothing in touch corresponds to the momentary retinal image, which serves as the input in most studies of vision, or to the spectrum of a continuous sound, which long played the same role in psychoacoustics. In active touch there are only continuously changing deformations of the skin, positions of the joints, velocities of the moving limbs, and other complexities. The very distinction between stimulus and response is uncertain: the observer moves his hand and perceives the object at the same time.

Finally, active touch cannot be imposed upon an experimental subject. Most studies of vision have involved subjects who sat perfectly still while the experimenter illuminated their retinae at his pleasure. Similarly, psychoacoustics has relied almost exclusively on studies in which precisely known waveforms were impressed upon the listener's ear by means of an earphone clamped to his head. The use of these passive techniques is not restricted to human subjects; animals or even parts of the nervous system can serve equally well. The concepts used in such research—thresholds, equivalent stimuli, receptive fields, and the like—are just as applicable to individual neurons in a sensory system as to real perceivers. Neither these methods nor these concepts are very helpful in the study of touch. To be sure, the skin of a passive animal can *be* touched or stimulated, and the subject can discriminate among stimuli thus applied. Research of this kind is occasionally done. It has commanded little enthusiasm, however, because "perception" under these conditions turns out to be far less accurate than when the perceiver can move about and explore his environment in a natural way.

The present view suggests a different approach to the problem. The claim that perception is a continuing process of exploration and information pickup, which may seem radical for vision, is self-evidently true for touch. The sequence of exploratory movement, information pickup, and further exploration can be directly observed whenever anyone examines an object manually. It is clear that haptic perception does not occur in any one instant and does not result from processing a single input. To be sure, we know very little about how it is done; we do not have adequate terms to describe the types of information that are available to the touch nor the types of movement that the observer must make to obtain them. But this is also true of vision, about which we know less than is generally supposed. We understand it only in artificially restricted situations and in terms of an oversimplified model.

Another important aspect of the perceptual cycle is especially obvious in the case of touch. Exploratory movements not only provide information about the object touched but also about the limb that touches it. Haptic information can specify both the shape of the thing being handled and the movements of the hands themselves. It will appear later, however (in Chapter 6) that this is equally true of vision. All perceptual activity provides information about the perceiver as well as the environment, about the ego as well as the world.

Listening

Listening is a temporally extended activity. Sound waves exist only in time; there is normally no single moment at which one hears. An initial burst of sound pressure can be detected, but we cannot listen to it. At the end of an acoustic sequence such as a train of footsteps or a spoken word, the listener has already been hearing it for some time; at the beginning he has not heard it at all.

Although hearing requires no exploratory movements like those of the eyes or hands, it is fundamentally the same sort of cyclic activity. (Even in vision, of course, eye movements are only an ordinary concomitant of schematic functioning, not a necessary one.[14]) The listener continuously develops more or less specific readinesses (anticipations) for what will come next, based on information he has already picked up. These anticipations—which themselves must be formulated in terms of temporal patterns, not of isolated moments—govern what he will pick up next, and in turn are modified by it. Without them, he would hear only a blooming, buzzing confusion.

All of us have schematic anticipations for the structured sounds of our own language; that is why we hear them as distinct and separate words while the talk of foreigners often appears to be an almost continuous stream. We develop such anticipations in the course of listening to any individual sentence; hence we can identify words far more easily in context than in isolation.[15] It is precisely this characteristic of speech perception that has made it so difficult to simulate mechanically. Even today, computers like HAL in "2001" remain in the realm of science fiction; no one has programmed any machine to understand more than a very limited range of speech.[16]

The anticipations of the listener, like those of the looker, are not highly specific. He does not know exactly what he will hear; otherwise why should he bother to listen? It would be a mistake to suppose that perceivers constantly formulate highly specific hypotheses about what is coming next and discard them in favor of better ones only when they fail to fit.[17] Perceptual hypotheses are rarely definite. At any given moment, what has already been picked up predicts the spatial origin and general nature of what will be obtained next, but does not define it precisely. Perception is hypothesis testing only in a very general sense. Perhaps, however, it is the most appropriate sense. The real guiding hypotheses of scientists are also of a general nature, directing exploration rather than prescribing exactly what will be found. The precise hypotheses postulated by some philosophers of science, ideally vulnerable to disconfirming evidence at every moment, play only a small part in the actual conduct of productive research.

Combining information in several modalities

The discussion so far has considered one modality at a time: vision, touch, hearing. This follows a long-established tradition. The invariable custom of books on perception is to treat each modality in one or more separate chapters. I did so myself in *Cognitive Psychology*,[18] following first visual and then auditory information inward from the stimulus through as many stages of processing as possible. Such an organization is natural in terms of the internal processing model. If we think of information as picked up by feature detectors, and processed into a percept, then a separate flow in each modality is obviously the simplest case. Consequently, it is the most studied case. Ninety-nine out of every 100 perception experiments (or perhaps 999 out of every 1,000) involve stimulation of only a single sense.

The facts of ordinary life are very different. Most events, at least those that interest us and to which we attend, stimulate more than one sensory system. We see someone walk and hear his footsteps, or hear him talk as we watch his face. We look at the things we handle, and experience our own body movements both kinesthetically and visually. In our mouths we feel what we taste, and sense the movements of the organs of speech as we hear the sound of the words we are speaking. In driving a car we feel its responsiveness to the controls as we watch its movement along the road; in observing an argument we see the gestures and attitudes of the participants as we hear their words and tones of voice.

This multiplicity of information is surely used in the act of perceiving. The schemata that accept information and direct the search for more of it are not visual or auditory or tactual, but perceptual. To attend to an event means to seek and accept every sort of information about it, regardless of modality, and to integrate all the information as it becomes available. Having heard something, we look to see it, and what we see then determines how we locate and interpret what we hear. Having seen something, we reach out to touch it, and what our hands feel is coordinated with what we see. If these coordinations were acquired late in life, as a result of extensive experience, students of basic perceptual processes might be justified in ignoring them. In fact, however, they probably occur in young infants as well as in adults. We pay attention to objects and events, not to sensory inputs. Although the next two chapters will focus primarily on vision, it is important to keep in mind that the perceptual cycle typically involves coordinated activity in several sensory systems at once.

Notes

1. I am ignoring the chemical senses—taste and smell—for the time being. Some speculations about taste will appear in Chapter 7.
2. Descartes (1638). I am familiar with this work only through secondary sources.
3. This terminology is J. J. Gibson's.
4. There is now so much material about neural detectors that it would be impossible to survey it adequately here. For a brief overview of this work and an example of the kind of theory that can be based on it, see Lindsay and Norman (1972).
5. Neisser (1967).
6. Some theorists (e.g., Segal, 1971a, 1972) have interpreted constructive theory to mean virtually this, and some incautious phrasing in my earlier book probably encouraged them to do so. I regret it, because such an interpretation leads rapidly to a sort of "perceptual relativism" in

which everyone's view of the world is by definition as accurate as everyone else's.

7. J. J. Gibson first proposed what he calls "ecological optics" in a 1961 paper, and elaborated it in *The Senses Considered as Perceptual System* (1966). He has developed it considerably further in a nearly completed manuscript entitled *An Ecological Approach to Visual Perception*, of which many draft chapters are available. In a paper to be published shortly (Neisser, in press) I attempt a somewhat more general analysis of Gibson's theory and its implications.

8. Not only can a regularly spaced grating of vertical bars be treated as a simple spatial waveform, but any unchanging optical pattern can be analyzed as a superimposition of such waveforms in two dimensions by means of Fourier analysis, just as any time-varying acoustic wave may be treated as a sum of sinusoids. This mode of analysis, introduced by Campbell and Robson (1968), has produced some remarkable results. See Sekuler (1974) for a recent review.

9. In addition to her systematic *Principles of Perceptual Learning and Development* (1969), E. J. Gibson has recently provided an elegant and forceful critique of the entire information-processing approach ("How Perception Really Develops," in press). For an important application of her theory, see E. J. Gibson and H. Levin, *The Psychology of Reading* (1975).

10. Some philosophers have been driven to postulate the existence of percepts by the fact that we sometimes seem to see things that aren't really there: motion pictures, after-images, double images, hallucinations, dreams, etc. Most of these cases involve a kind of "simulation"; that is, the perceiver is being systematically misinformed. Either the real environment or a part of his visual system is simulating an object by providing some of the information that would be available if the object were actually present. The mechanism of simulation is obvious for motion pictures, and hardly less obvious in the case of after-images, double images, and similar phenomena. Such

simulations are usually incomplete and easy to detect; we know a movie or an after-image when we see one. In these cases the "percept" might be defined as the particular object (or blurred form, etc.) that would most nearly provide the same information if it were actually present. When the object *is* present, there is no need to define a separate percept at all.

11. A similar view has been advanced independently and effectively by Hochberg (1970, 1975).

12. Bruner (1951, 1973); Gregory (1970, 1973).

13. The only substantial modern treatment of active touch known to me is J. J. Gibson's (1962).

14. Vision is still possible, though less effective, when eye movements are prevented by fixation instructions; see, for example, Littman and Becklen (in press).

15. Miller, Heise, and Lichten (1951).

16. The nearest approximation is the HEARSAY program, devised at Carnegie-Mellon University (Erman, 1975).

17. The mistake in question is my own. In 1967 I suggested, following Halle and Stevens (1964), that speech is perceived by "analysis-by-synthesis," meaning that the listener formulates a series of specific hypotheses about the message and then tests them on the sound wave. I no longer believe that this can be literally true; it would require that an implausibly large number of false hypotheses be generated all the time. The listener's active constructions must be more open and less specific, so that they are rarely disconfirmed.

18. Neisser (1967).

Ordinary Seeing

The concept of ecological validity has become familiar to psychologists.[1] It reminds them that the artificial situation created for an experiment may differ from the everyday world in crucial ways. When this is so, the results may be irrelevant to the phenomena that one would really like to explain. For example, studies of how rats learn mazes in the laboratory long failed to capture the learning abilities that the same animals display in their natural environment.[2] Similarly, studies of human memory using lists of nonsense syllables have not been helpful in explaining school learning or everyday remembering.[3]

In view of these bits of psychological history, the demand that experiments be ecologically valid appears to be a sensible one. However, that demand is not always as clear or helpful as it seems. Like so many admonitions to virtue, it emphasizes the superior righteousness of the moralizer without giving much guidance to the moralizee. Good experiments as well as poor ones differ from the everyday world, and good theories as well as bad ones have been built on such experiments. The situations of everyday life differ widely from one another; which one is to be imitated? Demands for ecological validity are only intelligible if they are specific. They must point to particular aspects of ordinary situations that are ignored by current experimental methods, and there must be good reason to suppose that those aspects are important. I believe that important aspects of the normal environment *are* being ignored in contemporary research paradigms. These aspects are the spatial, temporal, and intermodal continuities of real objects and events.

Contemporary studies of cognitive processes usually use stimulus material that is abstract, discontinuous, and only marginally real. It is almost as if ecological *in*validity were a deliberate feature of the experimental design. Subjects are shown isolated letters, words, occasionally line drawings or pictures, but almost never objects. These stimuli are not brought into view in any normal way. Usually they materialize in a previously blank field, and they often disappear again so soon that the viewer has no chance to look at them properly. They are drawn as if suspended magically in space, with no background, no depth, and no visible means of support. Consider the following excerpt from the method section of an influential study:

> The experimental equipment consisted of a Digital Equipment Corporation PDP-8 computer connected to a Tektronix Model 611 storage scope. The computer was programmed to display a series of

four visual fields on the scope, making it much like
a four-channel tachistoscope. The display scope and
response keys were in an experimental room separate from the computer and teletype. The subjects
were run individually, seated in front of a panel on
which the response keys were mounted. The display scope was positioned at eye level on a wheeled
cart behind a panel. This allowed the distance from
the subject to be adjusted so that the mask field
subtended an angle of 2½ degrees for each subject.
A 7½ watt night-light provided dim overall illumination for the experimental room, sufficient for the
dark-adapted subjects to see the response keys, yet
not so much that the subjects could see their reflec-
tion in the glass scope face. An intercom allowed
the experimenter in the computer room to com-
municate with the subject. . . . The sequence of
events during each trial was as follows: first the fixation point was displayed. Then the subject initiated
the trial by pressing a key with his left hand. The
fixation point disappeared, and the stimulus field
was displayed for the length of time specified
. . . (this varied for different subjects, but was of the
order of 25 or 50 milliseconds—UN). Immediately
after the offset of the stimulus the mask field was
displayed. The mask field consists of a random pattern of dots, different on each trial. After the choice
delay interval (possibly 0 seconds), the two choices
appeared to the right of the mask field. Both the
mask and the choice fields remained on until the
subject pressed one of the response keys. The average rate was approximately one trial per 5½
seconds.[4]

Such displays come very close to not existing at all.
They last for only a fragment of a second, and lack all
temporal coherence with what preceded or what will
follow them. They also lack any spatial link with their
surroundings, being physically as well as temporally

disconnected from the rest of the world. They cannot be touched, cannot be heard, and cannot be glanced at more than once. The subject is isolated, cut off from ordinary environmental support, able to do nothing but initiate and terminate trials that run their magical course whatever he may do. Although the data obtained under such conditions can serve as the basis of much ingenious theorizing, the resulting theories may mislead us. Experimental arrangements that eliminate the continuities of the ordinary environment may provide insights into certain processing mechanisms, but the relevance of these insights to normal perceptual activity is far from clear.

It is not lack of sophistication that leads psychologists to adopt such methods. They follow naturally from the internal processing notion of perception. In that view, visual perception begins when an image is formed on the retina, triggering neural impulses from the receptor cells. A complex flow of processes is thus initiated—a flow that culminates in the percept or perhaps even in the response. The task of psychologists is to understand this flow. As I wrote some years ago:

> Visual cognition, then, deals with the processes by which a perceived, remembered, and thought-about world is brought into being from as unpromising a beginning as the retinal patterns . . . the term "cognition" refers to all the processes by which the sensory input is transformed, reduced, elaborated, stored, recovered, and used.[5]

If it were true that visual activity begins with a retinal pattern and ends when the information in that retinal pattern has been "recovered and used," there would be good reason to experiment with brief and artificial displays. By precisely controlling the start of the percep-

tual process, such displays permit equally precise measurement of its duration. Ingenious theoretical devices,
involving the comparison of response latencies in various conditions, then allow the experimenter to test
hypotheses about internal mechanisms. If we consider
more commonplace examples of perception, however,
we will see that this basic assumption is rarely met.

Moving objects

Perceivable objects are not always at rest, and neither
are perceivers. The human perceptual system has
evolved to serve a mobile organism in a world that includes mobile objects. This fact is crucial for J. J. Gibson's account of perception as well as for the present
attempt to integrate his views with cognitive psychology. It has, however, received little emphasis in other
perceptual theories. The seductive analogy between
eye and camera has too often suggested that motion is
just a nuisance for which perceivers must compensate
as best they can. In fact, however, it produces invaluable information. This is most strikingly true when the
perceiver himself moves, as will appear in Chapter 6.
Here we will begin with simpler cases in which he is at
rest. They will serve to illustrate the continuous cyclic
character of perceptual activity that was diagrammed in
Figure 2.

Suppose you watch something moving: a running
animal or a thrown ball. Probably you will follow it with
your eyes; even babies a few days old can track a moving object under suitable conditions.[6] Successful tracking is a continuing activity. The motion of the object
over a given short stretch of time determines how the
eyes (and/or the head) must move if its images are to

remain centered on the foveae of the two eyes. The
necessary movement is made, and perhaps corrected, so
that still more information can be picked up about the
object and its trajectory. This allows tracking to continue, and so on. In this case perceiving is very obviously cyclical and extended in time.

Unless the moving object happens to be moving
through a cloudless sky, it necessarily passes in front of
other objects. Unless it happens to be transparent, it
necessarily occludes parts of these background objects
as it passes; they are then "dis-occluded" again as it
goes on. Thus parts of the background objects, or of
their surfaces, disappear regularly at the front edge of
the moving object and reappear in its wake. These optical transitions provide unambiguous information about
the relative positions of the objects in question; information that perceivers pick up. They specify relative
location even in the absence of every other cue.[7]
For the observer with appropriately tuned schemata,
object motion is thus an aid to perception rather than
a hindrance.

If the moving object turns or tumbles or has limbs that
shift their positions, more information becomes available. In such instances (which include virtually all naturally occurring motions), parts of the object occlude
and reveal other parts as it goes. The projected shapes
and sizes of its surfaces at the eye vary systematically;
projected angles grow or shrink or vanish. These
changes, too, are information that can be used. This
possibility was demonstrated by Wallach and O'Connell,[8] in their study of the "kinetic depth effect." (The
name is unfortunate because such optical flows specify
the shapes of things rather than their "depth," or distance from the observer.[9])

A particularly impressive demonstration of perception based on optical transformations is that of Gunnar Johansson.[10] Using a motion picture camera, he filmed people walking about in a darkened room with small light bulbs attached to their ankles, knees, shoulders, elbows, and wrists. A single frame of the film shows only a meaningless pattern of dots. When the full movie is shown, however, everyone sees people walking. This perception is not created by any momentary retinal input, nor even by the motions of isolated points.[11] Entire events are perceived over time. Far more detailed and specific optical flow patterns become available in the fully illuminated environment when things move; they are surely used in ordinary perceiving.

We shall see in Chapter 5 that it is easy to attend to one event and ignore another on the basis of kinetic patterns, even when both are equally available to the eye. An observer can follow one movement among many (with or without moving his eyes) as easily as a listener can follow one conversation and ignore another in a crowded room. What is seen depends on how the observer allocates his attention; i.e., on the anticipations he develops and the perceptual explorations he carries out.

Arriving objects

The examples considered so far have been cases in which the continuous and cyclic character of perception is particularly obvious. What happens when a new object enters the field of view for the first time? In laboratory studies this situation is usually achieved instantaneously, as the experimenter turns on a stimulus display. This is a poor approximation to what ordinarily happens in the world. Suppose, for example, that a visitor arrives in my office, where I am industriously at work on this manuscript. Is there any definable instant at which I have not yet perceived him, followed immediately by another at which a retinal image is fully available to be processed? Evidently there is not. In most cases I am engaged in some particular activity before he arrives, and at a certain moment I look toward the door. Why do I look? It is probably because I either heard him coming or caught a glimpse of some movement out of the corner of my eye, in peripheral vision. These two possibilities are functionally similar, even though one is intermodal and the other is not. Both provide information that is used to guide subsequent perceptual activity.

It is no evolutionary accident that babies are born with a tendency to look toward the sources of sounds, nor that the outer parts of the retina are sensitive to motion and change although they are poorly endowed for pattern vision. The sound of a footstep, like the first peripheral glimpse of a movement, is an effective guide to further exploration. In its own right, it indicates only that somebody is moving in a certain region of the environment. Nevertheless, it allows the perceiver to anticipate roughly what a glance in that direction might reveal. This "anticipation" is not a deliberate and conscious hypothesis, of course, but a general readiness for information of a particular kind. If the perceiver actually executes the exploratory glance, he embarks on the perceptual cycle; otherwise, he fails to perceive the object. In the latter case the initiating information may still have some effect on him (he may startle or blink or return with renewed determination to what he was doing before) but it will be minor and transient.

To see my visitor properly, then, I must swivel my
head and eyes around for a better look. In that better
look, the visitor's face will probably be imaged on the
central fovea of my eye. But perception is not complete
in that moment either; during the next few seconds I
will shift my gaze repeatedly as I look at him. Each
exploratory eye movement will be made as a consequence of information already picked up, in anticipation of obtaining more. I will not be aware of the
fixations or their sequence; only of the visitor himself.

Even without the contributions of hearing or
peripheral vision, my visitor would not find me perceptually unprepared. After all, he must appear in the
doorway. But I am in my office; I already know where
the doorway is, and what lies beyond it, just as I know
the location of other familiar objects. This means that I
can anticipate the distances and possible motions of any
arriving guest. Information about his location and
movements fits into a preexisting spatial schema, which
it then modifies. A visitor who entered through the wall
or materialized in the middle of the room would be
more like a ghost than a person. His ghostliness would
be the first thing I noticed about him and would color
everything I saw afterwards. Most psychologists do
not believe in ghosts, but they often experiment
with stimuli that appear just as mysteriously. This may
be a mistake; at the very least, it creates an unusual
situation.

Stationary objects

We can see stationary objects as well as moving ones.
Sitting undisturbed at my desk, I may decide to look at
something. I fixate it, and an appropriate image is

formed on my retina. Does a perceptual act begin in that instant and terminate a fraction of a second later in the depths of my brain?

If we pursue this particular example, a curious difficulty arises. Since I am in my own office, I have seen almost everything in it already. In a general way I know what and where all the surrounding objects are and how to look at them. If I look at something now it will be to examine it more carefully, to see features previously unobserved. The lamp on my desk has little vent holes around the top, for example; I never noticed them before. But I did know the approximate size, shape and position of the lamp, and especially *that it was a lamp.* That is, I had a schema for the lamp to begin with that directed my looking and accepted the new information the look made available. An existing pattern of readiness was modified by that information and it directed further looks that picked up still more. The perceptual cycle applies to this stationary example just as it does to the visitor in the doorway.

This is a case where perception is influenced by past experience, by "stored information." It is important to see exactly how and where such experience exerts its effect. It would be a mistake to suppose that I add information from memory to information in the stimulus to achieve a combined result, as the internal model of Figure 1 would suggest. The existing schema, which has been formed by earlier experience, *determines* what I pick up instead of adding to it. In terms of a distinction drawn by the Gibsons,[12] perceptual learning is a matter of "differentiation" and not of "enrichment."

The assertion that perception involves anticipation is easily misunderstood. It does *not* imply that I can see only what I expect to see. If someone had substituted another lamp without telling me about it, I would probably notice the change. My first glance would provide information that changed the schema and would direct further exploration of the new object. When a perceptual cycle is carried out normally, schemata quickly tune themselves to the information actually available. Perception is veridical.

These considerations may answer an objection that the reader has probably already formulated. People aren't always in familiar environments, and they often look at unfamiliar objects. Perception does not merely serve to confirm preexisting assumptions, but to provide organisms with new information. Although this is true, it is also true that without some preexisting structure, no information could be acquired at all. There is a dialectical contradiction between these two requirements: we cannot perceive *unless* we anticipate, but we must not see *only* what we anticipate. If we were restricted to isolated and separate glances at the world, this contradiction would prove fatal. Under such conditions we could not consistently disentangle what we see from what we expect to see, nor distinguish objects from hallucinations. This dilemma, which is fatal to the internal processing model of perception, can be resolved in the perceptual cycle. Although a perceiver always has at least some (more or less specific) anticipations before he begins to pick up information about a given object, they can be corrected as well as sharpened in the course of looking.

Expectancy effects

The upshot of the argument is that perception is directed by expectations but not controlled by them; it involves the pickup of real information. Schemata exert their effects by selecting some kinds of information rather than others, not by manufacturing false percepts or illusions. The old joke that the optimist sees the doughnut while the pessimist sees the hole does not imply that either is mistaken. It does suggest, however, that each of them will be confirmed in his mood by what he has seen. If the environment is rich enough to support more than one alternative view (and it usually is), expectations can have cumulative effects on what is perceived that are virtually irreversible until the environment itself changes. But environments do change, and thus loosen the grip of old ways of seeing. The interplay between schema and situation means that neither determines the course of perception alone.

There are many experimental demonstrations of selective perception in "rich" environments: i.e., situations that can support two or more obviously different perceptual cycles. In one familiar case, the several possibilities simply consist of different objects or events that happen to be available simultaneously: two voices or two visual displays are presented at once, and the subject attends to one rather than the other. These are studies of selective attention proper and will be considered in Chapter 5. Sometimes a given class of objects or messages affords information at several different levels of subtlety and complexity: these are opportunities for *perceptual learning*, for developing schemata rather than choosing between them. Finally, it may happen that a single object or event offers contradictory information: it could support two different perceptual cycles that cannot be integrated within the same schema. Such displays are called "ambiguous," and it is easy to influence the manner in which they are perceived. Verbal instructions and previous exposures strongly affect the perception of ambiguously drawn pictures;[13] social norms alter judgments of the range of an illusory motion;[14] experimenter bias influences subjects' judgments of the attractiveness of a pictured face.[15] Demonstrations of this kind only succeed when the stimuli are genuinely ambiguous; like the doughnut, they must offer information for more than one sort of schema. It is very difficult to create misperceptions of really unambiguous stimuli, and no such manipulation can be effective indefinitely.[16]

In their search for expectancy effects in perception, psychologists have frequently turned to the tachistoscope, which presents visual stimuli for controllable fractions of a second. When the subject is thus restricted to a single glance at a display, the normal perceptual cycle cannot take place. Under these conditions, the effects of set and expectation are powerful indeed. People can name a briefly flashed word or identify a briefly flashed picture far more easily when it is anticipated or plausible than when it is rare or out of context, and they often make errors based on their presuppositions. (Donald Broadbent once remarked that an Englishman who briefly glimpses a country scene with a painted signboard can always report the inscription "Trespassers Will Be Prosecuted.") Although the restricted nature of the tachistoscopic display makes much of the work done with it irrelevant to our discussion, the questions raised by this work have been of much concern to cognitive psychologists. Two of these questions will be considered briefly. First, is the expectancy effect perceptual or is it just a matter of response bias? Second, how can anything at all be seen in a brief flash if perception is a temporally extended activity?

The first question need not concern us long, since it implicitly assumes the validity of the internal processing model. If stimuli were really converted to percepts and eventually to responses by a linear processing sequence, it might make sense to ask where expectancy had its effect. Processes near the left side of Figure 1 could then be called perceptual, while those at the right would not. Even with this assumption the question has no single answer; Erdelyi[17] has recently argued that expectancy effects can occur at many points along this chain. But if perceiving is normally a cyclic flow of schema and information pickup, the entire distinction is pointless. Tachistoscopic experiments simply do not tap normal perceptual skills, and the term *perception* cannot be consistently applied to anything that occurs in them.

This interpretation explains why introspective reports in tachistoscopic studies are so confused. The observer is frequently uncertain whether he actually "saw" something (a word or a picture) or merely "inferred" that it must have been present. Often his report is demonstrably wrong. He may confidently claim to have seen something that wasn't presented at all[18] or report as a guess something that was actually based on stimulus information. Such a subject is trying, unsuccessfully, to relate his past experiences of genuine perception to the contrived situation in which he finds himself. To do so, he must fit language that was appropriate for a circular flow of activity (as in Figure 2) into the procrustean bed of Figure 1. He may do this willingly, if he happens to share the experimenter's linear theory of perception, but he cannot do it consistently.

Iconic storage

The second tachistoscope-inspired question is more serious. Information can be reported from displays that are extremely brief. *How* brief depends on the prevailing brightness and contrast; even a microsecond is enough under optimal conditions. (Consider how much you can see in a single flash of lightning.) Many studies have shown that this is possible because the transient, high-contrast retinal pattern is stored in relatively complete form at a peripheral level of the visual system. I once christened this form of storage the *icon*, and will continue this usage here.[19] The duration of the icon, which has been measured with various techniques, is about one-half to two seconds depending on particular visual conditions. It can be obscured or erased if new patterned stimuli are presented before it fades; these masking and metacontrast effects are complicated and will not be reviewed here.[20] There can be no doubt, in any case, that it is the existence of the icon that enables us to see brief tachistoscopic displays.

I think it was Norbert Wiener who asked his readers to imagine a mechanic with an artificial arm trying to repair an engine: is the arm a part of the machinery with which the mechanic is struggling, or a part of the mechanic who is working on the engine? There is a similar ambiguity about the icon: does it present information for the perceiver to see, or is it part of the perceiver who is doing the seeing? From a spectator's point of view, it is obviously inside the subject; introspectively, it is like something visible. The display has already been turned off, but appears to the subject as if it were still gradually fading. In his classic experiment, Sperling showed that a signal presented shortly after the end of the display can still direct the subject to attend to one part of the icon rather than another.[21] The result is that he can then remember the attended parts far beyond the iconic duration itself; he has extracted information about them as he would about a real scene at which he was looking. (At one time it was believed that this required verbal naming of the items in question, but it does not.[22])

Most cognitive theorists have sided with the subject rather than the spectator. That is, they treat the icon as if it were a picture, independent of the perceptual mechanisms that "look at it"; a first, separate, and unique stage of processing. This may be the best way to approach the problem, especially since Sackitt[23] has shown that the anatomical locus of iconic storage is probably in the retinal receptors themselves. The icon simply simulates, for the rest of the nervous system, the information that would be picked up if the real display were still on. Nevertheless, it can play little part in normal vision: by definition it does not exist while a given fixation continues, and it is destroyed by masking after every eye movement. Although the exact retinal arrangement of still unperceived forms may be briefly stored under tachistoscopic conditions, this storage is not persistent or robust enough to affect the perceptual cycle.

Notes

1. The term itself was coined by Brunswik (1956), though his usage was slightly different from the one that is popular today.
2. What I really have in mind is the contrast between the somewhat sterile work on maze learning, bar pressing, etc. done by American psychologists a generation ago and the detailed observations of animals in their natural habitats conducted independently by European etholo-

gists. But the most striking single example for the rat has a different origin: it is Garcia's discovery (Garcia, Ervin, and Koelling, 1966) that rats avoid foods that have made them ill, even when hours elapse between the stimulus (tasting the food) and the reinforcement (becoming ill). For a recent review, see Seligman and Hager (1972).

3. This is a restrained understatement; nonsense-syllable learning is probably the archetype of psychological irrelevance. Yet that stereotype is no longer entirely deserved because the field has recently undergone a kind of Copernican revolution. Where formerly it was thought that rote-memory experiments would yield fundamental principles applicable elsewhere, the same methods are now used to study skills and strategies originally learned in the world and brought to the laboratory by the subject—imaging, categorizing, storytelling, etc.

4. Wheeler (1970, pp. 65-66).

5. Neisser (1967, p. 4).

6. Wolff and White (1965).

7. Kaplan (1969).

8. Wallach and O'Connell (1953).

9. J. J. Gibson has pointed out that the very notion of "depth perception" is misguided. What we see is a layout of objects at various distances from each other and from us. Almost all of them rest on the ground or are attached to something else that does. Our own position in this environment is perceptible as well. What psychologists have called "depth"—the length of the Berkeleyan line of sight between the eye and the object—has no special status in perception.

10. Johansson (1973); Maas and Johansson (1972).

11. Retinal "motion detectors" do not explain this kind of perception, though I am sure they play a role in it. The perceived direction of motion (including directions away from the observer) depends on the entire configuration.

12. J. J. Gibson and E. J. Gibson (1955). See also E. J. Gibson (in press).

13. The wife and mother-in-law figure is frequently used in

such demonstrations, but many other ambiguous figures are available. Some of this work is reviewed in my 1967 book.

14. Sherif (1935).

15. Rosenthal (1966), Chapter 9.

16. This is more nearly a definition than an empirical fact, since we define ambiguity by the possibility of alternative perceptions. I only mean to stress that it is more difficult to fool people than psychologists often suppose.

17. Erdelyi (1974).

18. Pillsbury (1897).

19. Neisser (1967).

20. For reviews of visual masking and metacontrast, see Kahneman (1968), Lefton (1973), or Turvey (1973).

21. Sperling (1960).

22. Scarborough (1972); Coltheart (1972).

23. Sakitt (1975).

Schemata

Perceiving is not the only activity that depends on spatial and temporal continuities. Actions and movements have the same character, and it is particularly obvious in every kind of skilled performance. The sculptor begins with some notion of what the finished statue is to be like; the tennis player with an idea of how the ball is to move after he hits it. Starting with this idea and also with the objective state of affairs—the block of stone to be worked, the present movements of the ball and the player himself—each of them acts, perceives the consequences of his actions, develops a more precise notion of what is to be done, acts again, perceives again, and so on until the final product is achieved. At each moment the skilled activity depends on the existing state of affairs, on what has gone before, and on the plans and expectations of the performer. This cyclic process fits the paradigm of Figure 2. Bartlett catches some of its flavor in a much-quoted passage:

> Suppose I am making a stroke in a quick game, such as tennis or cricket. How I make the stroke depends on the relating of certain new experiences, most of them visual, to other immediately preceding visual experiences, and to my posture, or balance of postures, at the moment. The latter, the balance of postures, is the result of a whole series of earlier movements, in which the last movement before the stroke is played has a predominant function. When I make the stroke I do not, as a matter of fact, produce something absolutely new, and I never merely repeat something old. The stroke is literally manufactured out of the living visual and postural "schemata" of the moment and their interrelations.[1]

A skilled performer is a part of the world; he acts on it and it acts on him. Perception is also a skill. It differs from performances like sculpting and tennis playing in that the perceiver's effects on the world around him are negligible; he does not change objects by looking at them or events by listening to them. (There are exceptions, of course, especially in the submicroscopic world of the physicist, but they do not concern us here.) In most other respects, however—in its continuity, its cyclic nature, its dependence on continuously modified schemata—perceiving is a kind of doing.

A definition

This book is not about doing but about perceiving and other cognitive activities. It is not the proper place to defend or elaborate the view that action is organized just like perception, guided by expectancies that in turn are altered by consequences. Such a defense would have to begin by citing a great deal of history. A generation ago, the primary dispute between "stimulus-response" and "cognitive" theories of animal learning was about whether behavior was controlled by reinforcement or expectancy. I now believe that both sides were right in that dispute, just as I believe that both J. J. Gibson and the hypothesis-testing theorists are right about perception. Indeed, there is a striking parallel between these theoretical confrontations. Gibson, like the radical behaviorists, hopes to explain activity purely in terms of the structure of the environment; all hypothetical explanatory constructs (including "schema"!) seem dangerously mentalistic. Extreme versions of information processing or constructive theories, on the other hand, pay little heed to the kind of information the environment actually offers. They leave the perceiver lost in his own processing system, just as the older cognitive theories were said to "leave the rat lost in thought in the maze." Perhaps if the present attempt to reconcile these views in terms of the perceptual cycle has any merit, it may suggest how to reconcile the older questions about behavior as well.

Although perceiving does not change the world, it does change the perceiver. (So does action, of course.) The schema undergoes what Piaget calls "accommodation," and so does the perceiver. He has become what he is by virtue of what he has perceived (and done) in the past; he further creates and changes himself by what he perceives and does in the present. "Existence precedes essence," as the existentialists say. Every person's possibilities for perceiving and acting are entirely unique, because no one else occupies exactly his position in the world or has had exactly his history.

There seems to be no better word than Bartlett's *schema* for the central cognitive structure in perception. (Bartlett was not entirely happy with it[2] and neither am I.) Because the term has already been used rather widely with a variety of meanings[3], I will try to define what I mean as explicitly as possible. A schema is that portion of the entire perceptual cycle which is internal to the perceiver, modifiable by experience, and somehow specific to what is being perceived. The schema accepts information as it becomes available at sensory surfaces and is changed by that information; it directs movements and exploratory activities that make more information available, by which it is further modified.

From the biological point of view, a schema is a part of the nervous system. It is some active array of physiological structures and processes: not a center in the brain, but an entire system that includes receptors and afferents and feed-forward units and efferents. Within the brain itself there must be entities whose activities account for the modifiability and organization of the schema: assemblages of neurons, functional hierarchies, fluctuating electrical potentials, and other things still unguessed. It is not likely that this physiological activity is characterized by any single direction of flow or unified temporal sequence. It does not just begin at the periphery and eventually arrive at some center, but must include many kinds of reciprocating and lateral patterns. Nor does it all begin at one moment and end at another; the continuities of different subsystems overlap in varying ways, providing for a host of different kinds of "information storage." It is important, but excruciatingly difficult, to understand these structures in biological terms. My present aim, however, is to understand them in relation to the perceptual cycle of which they are only a part. Perception involves the world as well as the nervous system.

Some analogies

The functions of schemata may be clarified by some analogies. In one sense, when it is viewed as an information-accepting system, a schema is like a *format* in a computer-programming language. Formats specify that information must be of a certain sort if it is to be interpreted coherently. Other information will be ignored or will lead to meaningless results. The advance specification need not be sharply limited, however. As noted earlier, schemata can operate at various levels of generality. You may be ready to see "something over there," or "somebody," or your brother-in-law George, or a smile on George's face, or even a cynical smile on George's face.

A schema is not merely like a format; it also functions as a *plan*, of the sort described by Miller, Galanter, and Pribram in their seminal book.[4] Perceptual schemata are plans for finding out about objects and events, for obtaining more information to fill in the format. One of their important functions in seeing is to direct exploratory movements of the head and eyes. But the schema determines what is perceived even where no overt movements occur (listening is a good example), because information can be picked up only if there is a developing format ready to accept it. Information that does not fit such a format goes unused. Perception is inherently selective.

The analogy between schemata and formats and plans is not complete. Real formats and plans incorporate a sharp distinction between form and content, but this is not true of schemata. The information that fills in the format at one moment in the cyclic process becomes a part of the format in the next, determining how further information is accepted. The schema is not only the plan but also the executor of the plan. It is a pattern *of* action as well as a pattern *for* action.

The activities of schemata are not contingent on any external sources of energy. If the right sort of information is available, the schema will accept it and may direct movements to search for more. But organisms have many schemata, related to each other in complex ways. Extensive schemata typically have less wide ones embedded in them, as we shall see in Chapter 6. When they do, the larger schema often determines, or "motivates," the activity of those embedded within it. Motives are not alien forces that bring otherwise passive systems to life; they are just more general schemata, that accept information and direct action on a larger scale. It is worth noting, too, that the activities directed by two schemata can come into conflict, or even be entirely incompatible. What happens then is called *selective attention;* and it will be treated in Chapter 5.

The schema at any given moment resembles a *genotype* rather than a *phenotype,* as these concepts are defined in genetics. It offers a possibility for development along certain lines, but the precise nature of that development is determined only by interaction with an environment. It would be a mistake to identify the schema with what is perceived, just as it is a mistake to identify any gene with a definite characteristic of an adult organism. Perception is determined by schemata somewhat in the same sense that the observable proper-

ties of organisms are determined by their genes: it results from the interaction of schema and available
information. Indeed, it is that interaction.

In an earlier book, I insisted that perception is a
"constructive process."[5] The perceiver is active. To a
considerable extent he chooses what he will see, selecting some objects for attention and perceiving some of
their properties rather than others. This is surely true,
but it may be wise to avoid the connotation that there is
a final, constructed product in the perceiver's mind;
that we see internal representations rather than real objects. This, I think, is not true. By constructing an anticipatory schema, the perceiver engages in an act that
involves information from the environment as well as
his own cognitive mechanisms. He is changed by the
information he picks up. The change is not a matter of
making an inner replica where none existed before, but
of altering the perceptual schema so that the next act
will run a different course. Because of these changes,
and because the world offers an infinitely rich texture of
information to the skilled perceiver, no two perceptual
acts can be identical.

Frames

A discussion of the concept of schema cannot ignore
two influential notions that bear at least a family re-
semblance to it. One, developed by Marvin Minsky,
is applicable to artificial intelligence and robotics;[6]
the other is due to the sociologist Erving Goffman.[7]
Curiously, both have the same name: *frames*. Although
they have little in common superficially, both attempt

to recognize the crucial role of context and meaning in cognitive activity. (A new stress on context is appearing in other areas of psychology as well, from memory[8] to the socialization of the child.[9] This may be a sign that the social sciences are at last coming to grips with the complexly embedded characteristics of ordinary human life.)

By now, the attempt to program computers to carry out pattern recognition has a relatively long history. There have been impressive developments in the last few years. For example, several existing systems make it possible for a computer to describe the full three-dimensional layout of a jumbled pile of blocks, each with a different and unforeseen shape, simply on the basis of a frontal photograph of the scene that has been scanned by an input device.[10] Nevertheless, Minsky (in whose laboratory much of this work was done) has come to believe that adequate recognition and description of scenes in the real world will never be possible on the basis of momentary input patterns alone. He proposes that the computer must be ready for each new scene with a frame, or a hierarchy of frames, that anticipates much of what will appear. If the computer is examining a room, it should expect to find walls, doors, windows, furniture, and so forth; only in this way will it be able to interpret the otherwise ambiguous information available to it. He supposes that such a system will make "default assignments" in the absence of information, hypothesizing the existence of a right-hand wall, for example, even if it has not yet received any relevant evidence.

Minsky's view has a good deal in common with the one being presented here. There are substantial differences, but it would be a digression to explore them.[11]

Such a convergence between artificial intelligence and cognitive psychology is heartening, even though (so far as I know) no significant computer program based on the frame theory has yet been written.

Goffman uses the term "frame" very differently. In a brilliant analysis of the events of everyday social life, he points out how often they are set in conventionally established frames that alter or transform their meaning. His central example is theatrical performance, in which the onlookers know that the speeches and actions they observe must not be taken at face value but in some other way. Ordinary life is full of similar phenomena. The same words of praise may be genuine on one occasion, ironic on another, or an account of someone else's remarks in a third; too much drinking may be framed as illness by some perceivers, deliberate wickedness by others; political organizations hold meetings for the sole purpose of being televised (i.e., exhibited in a certain frame); swindlers create carefully framed situations for their dupes to misunderstand. If psychology is ever to deal seriously with the perception of ordinary events, it will have to confront the complexities Goffman describes. In many respects, his attempt to analyze the perceptible social world is parallel to J. J. Gibson's ecological optics, which analyzes the perceptible physical environment and the information it provides.

Information pickup
and information storage

The notion of picking up information is central to my argument as well as Gibson's. Can it be reconciled with the classical view of information as something that can be quantified, transmitted, stored, and processed?[12] I believe that the two usages are compatible,[13] but the relationship between them needs explication.

By Shannon's definition, information is essentially a selection among alternatives. It exists whenever some given system is in one possible state rather than in another. Information has been *transmitted* (by definition) when the state of one system, B, is somehow contingent on the state of another, A, so that in principle an observer could discover something about A by examining B. If enough information has been transmitted to B (without noise) A can be characterized in great detail. Exactly this relation exists between the structured pattern of light available to the eye (B) and the objects from which it has been reflected (A). Information about the objects is in the light, because the laws of optics create a contingency between them. (This contingency is usually perfect, free of what information theorists call "noise.") The information in the light specifies the layout and many of the properties of environmental objects. J. J. Gibson maintains that in the normal environment this specification is unique: no other imaginable world could give rise to the optical structure that actually exists. (Optical structure here includes changes over time as well as distributions in space.)

The perceiver is also a physical system, in contact with the optic array. His state is partially determined by the structure of that array, which means that information is transmitted to him. When this happens—when his nervous system acquires structure from the light—we say that he has picked up information. If this information—the aspects of optical structure by which he is affected—itself specifies the real properties of objects, he has perceived those properties and objects.

Information pickup requires an appropriate perceptual system—appropriate in the sense that its state can
be usefully altered by contact with the structured light.
It is commonly argued that this system (here called the
schema) must *process* the information available to it.
This term may be misleading. The information itself is
not changed, since it was in the light already. The
schema picks it up, is altered by it, uses it. Some of
those activities may indeed be captured by the many
contemporary studies that have the concept of information processing (or *recoding*) as their theoretical
rationale. Nevertheless, I will not review them here.
There are simply too many of them to cover in a volume
such at this, and other reviews are available.[14] Most
such studies are based on artificially contrived situations like those described earlier, neglecting the continuous and cyclic character of ordinary perceptual
activity. Moreover, almost all of them begin with one
particular scientific description of the stimulus information, which is considered as an array of separately
stimulating rays of light. Given such a description,
theories of perception can only be of a certain kind, and
must postulate fundamental processes of transformation
and recoding. However, that description is surely not
the only possible one. Just as acoustic information can
be described either in pressure-wave or frequency-
spectrum terms, so there must also be various equivalent descriptions of the structure of the optic array. As
noted in Chapter 2, several alternatives are now being
developed.

There is still another reason for skepticism about contemporary accounts of our perceptual machinery. The
machinery does not come into existence all at once.
Schemata develop with experience. Information pickup

is crude and inefficient at first, as are the perceptual explorations by which the cycle is continued. Only through perceptual learning[15] do we become able to perceive progressively more subtle aspects of the environment. The schemata that exist at any given moment are the product of a particular history as well as of the ongoing cycle itself. No theory that fails to acknowledge the possibility of development can be taken seriously as an account of human cognition.

The existence of perceptual learning implies that the state of the schema at any given time, A_1, is somehow contingent on its state at an earlier time, A_0. Given the definition of information transmission, it would be legitimate to say that information has been "transmitted" from A_0 to A_1. It is much less awkward, however, to say that it has been "preserved" or "stored." Thus schemata not only enable us to perceive present events but also to store information about past ones.

The concept of stored information plays a key role in most contemporary theories of memory. It has often been suggested that the brain functions essentially like a large library system.[16] In that view, traces of individual past experiences are stored in the library stacks (long-term memory) and occasionally retrieved for conscious reexamination. If the librarian fails to locate them, forgetting occurs. Whatever the merits of this view may be, it is not what I mean here. Someone who "has" a currently inactive schema should not be thought of as the owner of a particular kind of mental property. He is just an organism with a particular potentiality. His inactive schemata are not objects but aspects of the structure of his nervous system. Although they preserve information in the technical sense, it is not picked up as if it were information in the light. It is just manifested by the specificity of his anticipation when a schema is used.

Origins of the perceptual cycle

If the present account of perception is correct, there can never have been a time when we were altogether without schemata. The newborn infant opens his eyes onto a world that is infinitely rich in information: he has to be ready for some of it if he is to engage in the perceptual cycle and become ready for more.

It seems necessary, then, to credit even the youngest baby with a certain amount of innate perceptual equipment—not merely with sense organs but with neural schemata to control them. At the same time, we must not credit him with too much. The ancient platonic idea that all knowledge is innate seems entirely inadequate to the changing human condition. People have to learn about the world; they do not know what it will be like in advance, and they never know all about it no matter how diligent and perceptive they may be. What babies do know, I believe, is how to find out about their environment, and how to organize the information they obtain so it can help them obtain more. They do not know even this very well, but well enough to begin.

There is a good deal of experimental evidence on this point. Infants carry out many kinds of information gathering activity; they are engaged in the perceptual cycle from the first. They look toward sounds, follow objects with their eyes, and reach out toward things that they see. The case of looking toward sounds is particularly interesting, because this behavior appears very

early. Even a newborn baby, only a few minutes old,
often moves his eyes toward a source of sound and
rarely moves them in the wrong direction.[17]

We need not assume that such an infant knows the
location of the sound source with any precision. The
fact that he looks toward it shows only that he can tell
whether it is to the right or the left. These two possibilities are distinguished by the ear at which the
sound arrived first: by a *time-difference* between the
acoustic patterns at his two ears. The direction of the
time-difference is enough to specify a rightward or left-
ward origin, while its actual magnitude can specify the
location of the source much more exactly. This more
precise specification is not absolute, however. It depends on the distance between the listener's ears; i.e.,
on the size of his head. Since head size changes by a
factor of two during growth, it is hard to see how precise
auditory localization could be preprogrammed innately.

A few days after birth, a newborn baby has enough
control over his neck muscles to move his head as well
as his eyes toward a source of sound. If the sound continues as he does so, his head movement will change
the very time-difference between the ears that initiated
it. When he has turned far enough to face the sounding
object, the difference will have become zero. In this
way, he effectively localizes the sound without taking
his head size into account after all! Repetitions of this
activity can eventually teach him how large a head
movement is needed to nullify any initial difference. In
effect, he can "calibrate" his own head size. When he
has done so, his ability to localize sounds will be much
more satisfactory. The same activities will serve to keep
his localization accurate in spite of changing head size
as he grows older.[18]

For the infant, then, perceiving the direction of a source of sound is a perceptual act, cyclically extended in time. This act contains the seeds of its own further development, as the schema becomes increasingly specific. At first a wide range of signals—sounds coming from anywhere on the right—are accepted as equivalent, and produce the same imprecise movements of eye or head. Later, a more articulated schema picks up information about the particular direction in which the sound source lies, and controls a correspondingly more precise response. The development of the schema is therefore from the general to the particular, from undifferentiated to precise. But although this is the course of cognitive growth for schemata, it is not what happens to the perceptual acts themselves. The perceptual cycle is concrete and specific from the beginning. The baby's head movement toward the sound source is perfectly definite, albeit slow, because a single definite source really exists. Perception is always an interaction between a particular object or event and a more general schema. It can be regarded as a process of generalizing the object or of particularizing the schema depending on one's theoretical inclinations.

The view of cognitive development being presented here evidently has much in common with that of Piaget. In particular, the perceptual cycle is not unlike the "circular reaction" he describes.[19] An infant who somehow produces an environmental effect (e.g., by touching a toy that makes a noise) tends to repeat his act over and over again with obvious pleasure. Although the perceptual cycle need not involve overt activity of this sort—looking and listening are just as cyclic as touching—it certainly does in many instances. Moreover, many important kinds of information can only be obtained

manually; the child may never discover the rattle's
characteristic sound or the hardness of its surface without touching it. These cyclic interactions modify the
initial schema, a process Piaget calls *accommodation.*

Although accommodation certainly occurs, Piaget's
companion concept of *assimilation* seems more dubious. Why should we suppose that the child alters the
information he picks up? He finds out less about his
environment than an adult would, but what he does
discover need not be wrong. While he makes mistakes,
as we all do, these may be incorrect extrapolations from
what he has seen rather than fundamental illusions.
Piaget's "conservation" task illustrates this point. When
a five-year-old insists that there is no longer the same
amount of water after it has been poured from a tall thin
glass to a short wide one, it is because he does not yet
know what sort of information accurately specifies
amount. (That is, of course, another way of saying that
he does not have the adult concept of quantity.) He
must make do with the information he has, which in this
case specifies only the height of the water in its vessel,
and so he makes an error. He does not err because he is
at an inevitably illogical stage of cognitive development, but because he has not looked attentively at
events of this kind often enough to develop the
schemata that the problem demands. Children who
have had relatively more experience with the critical
substance and its transformations make fewer conservation errors.[20]

Perceptual development does not occur automatically, innately, regardless of the environment. The
cycle of anticipation and pickup links the perceiver to
the world, and can only develop along avenues that the
world offers. Pygmies who live in dense tropical forests,

where distant objects are rarely visible, are said to make ludicrous mistakes when they first see a herd of animals far away.[21] Similarly, inexperienced outfielders make gross defensive errors by misjudging the flight of the ball, and new drivers anxiously wonder whether their cars will fit into huge parking spaces. With practice, such skills develop to a point that seems magical to the uninitiated.

Infants engage in many kinds of perceptual exploration other than those that have been considered here. From the very beginning, they choose to look at novel rather than familiar objects; often the mere presentation of something new is enough to induce the state of "alert inactivity" which indicates that they have become interested in their environment. They prefer moving objects to stationary ones, perhaps because movement offers so much additional information, and they may prefer noisy objects to silent ones for the same reason. They move their eyes to fixate new objects presented in the periphery of the field of view, and they track moving objects if the motion is not too fast for them. By the age of four or five months, if not before, they reach out to touch what they can see and try to bring grasped objects into view.

There has been considerable discussion about whether very young infants have an "object concept." Does a baby know that toys and people continue to exist even when they have gone out of sight, or does he think of them as phantasms produced only by his own perceptual activity? This is an unfortunate phrasing of the question, which originates with philosophers rather than infants. Young children surely do not make generalizations of either kind. They have anticipatory schemata: the question is what kinds of information they anticipate, and how long they continue to do so without the support of continuously available information. With regard to the first of these issues, the empirical evidence is clear. Spelke, for example, presented two movies on adjacent screens to 3-month-old babies and played the sound track corresponding to one of the films through a centrally-located loudspeaker: the babies looked mostly at the film which corresponded to the available auditory information.[22] Even the earliest exploratory activity is evidently intermodal, coordinating the activities of the eyes, ears, and hands. Infants expect to see the things they have heard and touched, and to touch the things they have seen. Indeed, they may be startled when these expectations are not confirmed.[23] In this respect, then, their object concept resembles that of adults. Their schemata are well attuned to the real nature of things in the world, which are in fact accessible to several of our senses.

Evidence for the persistence of perceptual anticipations has been more equivocal. Such persistence can be inferred either from the surprise an infant displays when a temporarily concealed object fails to reappear, or from his efforts in searching for something that is no longer in view. Studies in which objects are temporarily concealed have yielded positive results. In some of T. G. R. Bower's experiments,[24] a screen briefly covers up a toy at which the baby has been looking; when it moves away again the toy is gone because the experimenter has secretly removed it. If the occlusion lasts only a second or two, even a one-month-old baby is surprised that the toy is no longer there (judging, at least, by the fact that his heart rate changes). On the other hand, he is not surprised if some other toy appears in its place; he anticipates seeing something, but without regard to the detail information that distinguishes one object from another. Apparently he does not maintain his anticipation very long—after a 15-second occlusion he is more surprised if the toy is still there than if it is gone. Older infants show evidence of continuing expectation over longer intervals of time.

The things a baby perceives in this persistent and multi-sensory way are surely not mere "sensations." When he looks at a cube, he does not see a flat and foreshortened picture like the optical projection of the cube in his eye, but an object that has size, solidity, and location. (The fact that some attributes go unnoticed does not make the object seem incomplete, of course. Properties we don't notice are like ideas we have not had. They leave no gap in the world; it takes information to specify gaps.) Having rejected the notion that an adult has an inner homunculus to look at retinal images, we must not make the same mistake where the baby is concerned. The child may be father of the man, but there is no inner child to father an inner man. The child does not see his retina; he sees because the complex patterns of light available there provide information about objects. Those patterns specify solidity, real shape and size to the adult: why should they not for the infant?[25]

The schema that an infant maintains after an object has gone out of sight may prepare him for its reappearance, but it does not necessarily enable him to find the object again by himself. Infants display odd patterns of visual and manual search. Sometimes they give up too easily: a six-month-old baby makes no effort to remove a cloth that has been draped over an attractive toy. On other occasions, they persevere in an obviously maladaptive way: a three-month-old can follow a repeti-

tive motion with his head and eyes but fails to change
his looking pattern when the object takes a new
course;[26] one-year-olds exhibit a similar rigidity in
searching for a hidden object even if they have seen it
put in a new place.[27]

Observations like these have generally been interpreted as indicating a deficiency in the child's object
concept.[28] He is said to believe that the object has
ceased to exist when it is covered,[29] or that it becomes a
new and different object whenever it moves.[30] These
hypotheses seem unnecessarily dramatic. The data indicate only that infants are relatively unskilled in the art
of locating things that have gone out of sight and sometimes put so much faith in a newly-acquired search
strategy that they overlook the obvious. As an occasionally absent-minded professor who has been known to
check the same location over and over again because a
lost object really ought to be there, I have a good deal of
sympathy for the subjects of these experiments. Their
basic object concept may be no more deficient than
mine; it's just that they are even worse than I am at
finding things.

Meaning and categorization

In one respect, discussions of the object concept are
bound to be misleading no matter what theoretical view
eventually prevails. They implicitly suggest that the
function of perception is to inform us about things as
mere objects: geographically and physically defined
hunks of matter that are what they are whether we look
at them or not. This is true, but it is far from being the
whole truth. In the normal environment most percepti-

ble objects and events are *meaningful*. They afford various possibilities for action, carry implications about
what has happened or what will happen, belong coherently to a larger context, possess an identity that
transcends their simple physical properties. These
meanings can be, and are, perceived. One can see that a
facial movement is a cynical smile, that the object on
the desk is a pen, that there is a door over there under
the EXIT sign. In reading or in listening, one perceives
the meaning of words and sentences, the drift of an
argument, or the undertone of feeling that may be
represented. These perceptions often seem very direct,
in the sense that we become aware of the meanings
without seeming to notice the physical details that provide evidence for them. At least we are often unable to
describe these details (what defines a cynical smile?),
and we forget them quickly even when they are potentially describable (did the sentence above say "*One* can
see . . ." or "*We* can see . . . that a facial movement is a
cynical smile?").

This aspect of perception has long been a theoretical
stumbling block for psychology. It has seemed that
stimuli themselves cannot possibly have meaning, because they are merely patterns of light or sound or pressure. The meaning must be supplied by the perceiver
after he has registered the stimuli. Why, then, do introspective reports suggest that the meaning is available
first, and the stimulus details only later or not at all?
Early experimental psychologists tried to solve the
problem by decree: any introspective report of a perceived meaning was simply a mistake, the *stimulus error*, which properly trained subjects ought to avoid. This
remarkable attempt to dictate what introspection should
reveal proved a failure and was abandoned, but the

problem remained. It is particularly acute in internal information processing models like Figure 1. A glance at the figure shows that information is necessarily meaningless when it arrives at the "sensory register." Meaning is added only later, by contributions from memory.

J. J. Gibson attempts to deal with the perception of meaning through the concept of *affordance*.[31] All the potential uses of objects—the activities they afford— are said to be directly perceivable. Invariant properties of the optic array specify that the floor affords walking, the pen affords writing, and so on. These aspects of optical structure are different from those that specify position or shape or motion, but they are no less objective and in no way derivative. The difficulty with this formulation is that what an object appears to afford—or to mean—depends on who is perceiving it. Every natural object has a vast number of uses and potential meanings, and every optic array specifies an indefinite variety of possible properties. The perceiver selects among these properties and affordances, by virtue of specific readinesses for some and not for others. Perception of meaning, like the perception of other aspects of the environment, depends on schematic control of information pickup.

If perceiving is a cyclical activity of the kind illustrated in Figure 2, we need not assign meaning to either the environment or the perceiver alone, nor be disturbed that it comes to consciousness before (or without) the physical properties on which it allegedly depends. It takes time to perceive *any* aspect of an object, whether it be the meaning of your brother-in-law George's smile or the relative lengths of his mouth and his eyebrows. Your schemata develop differently in those two cases, and you execute different exploratory eye movements that make different information available. In one case you look for and find additional facial evidence of smiling, certain patterns of movement that characterize smiles over time, and—over longer periods—more actions by George that reflect the same feelings on his part. In the other case, you might look for information specifying, say, whether the ends of his mouth reach nearer to the edge of his face than the eyebrows do. Whether you see the meaning of a smile or just its shape depends on which sort of cycle you are engaged in, not on any single instantaneous input and its processing in your head. Neither of these kinds of perception (and there are indefinitely many kinds of perception in this sense) is logically prior to the other. The geometric one does not occur at a lower level of processing than the meaningful one, nor is there any reason to suppose that it occurs earlier in the perceptual development of the child. Indeed, the opposite is more likely, as we will see in Chapter 9.

Although this account of the perception of meaning applies to the ordinary, temporally extended case, it can also be verified in tachistoscopic experiments. Generalized, meaning-defined schemata can function even under the adverse conditions of a brief and un-explorable display, or a forced rapid visual search. Many such experiments have demonstrated the efficacy of perceptual sets defined by meaning, use, or conventional category. In one study, a pictorial target was defined for subjects either by actually being shown or just by a verbal description ("Two men drinking beer"). Both definitions were equally effective in helping them identify the picture later when it was presented among many others in a rapid sequence.[32] In another experimental paradigm, subjects must look through sentences or strings of words for a target defined literally (PEAR), acoustically ("pair"), or by meaningful category (a fruit); the definition by category usually results in the fastest performance.[33] Finally, it has often been shown that subjects can pick out a particular number more easily from an array of irrelevant letters than from among other numerals.[34] This is true even when the target is the character "0", defined as a letter on some trials and as the numeral zero on others.[35] There is a perceptual schema for *number* that accepts information independently of, and perhaps more rapidly than, the schemata for individual numbers. Of course, the use of categorial schemata does not always lead to improved performance; it can also produce gross errors in reports of tachistoscopic displays.[36]

The process of assigning objects or stimuli to categories is properly called *pattern recognition,* and many theories of this process have been advanced in recent years.[37] The chief problem for these theories has been the mechanism of classification itself: does one identify a chair as a chair by detecting the presence of certain critical features, by matching the input to a prototypical template for chairs, or perhaps by synthesizing an internal model of a chair and matching it to the stimulus? The issue may not be decidable: my present guess is that each of these mechanisms is used in at least some classificatory tasks by at least some subjects. In any case, it is important to realize that theories of pattern recognition are not necessarily theories of perception.

Perceiving is not a matter of assigning objects to categories. Because it depends on a flux of stimulation that changes uniquely over time, the development of the schema on any particular occasion is also unique. We don't just have a smile schema to fit every smile or a chair schema for every chair. Although no discussion of perception can proceed without using abstract concepts like *smile* and *chair*, which apply equally well to a thousand individual instances, the perceiver does not ordinarily use them himself. Just as there is no single moment when I see the chair, so there may be none when I recognize it as a chair. I probably will not categorize it at all unless the situation somehow requires that I do so. I can sit down in it, avoid it, move it out of the way, look for my missing pipe in its cushions, or notice that it clutters up the room too much without ever naming it at all, to others or to myself. While some of these activities might be said to categorize it "implicitly," each does so in a unique and different way.

In most cases we are unaware of the fine structure of our own perceptual activity. We do not usually note the successive views of an object that eye movements provide or the individual pressures at the skin that occur as we explore it with our hands: what we experience is the object. Similarly, we are aware of the meanings and affordances that the perceptual cycle reveals, not of the detailed phases of the cycle itself. What we later remember is also the object (or event) and its meanings, or more precisely the occasion of our perceiving them. What we remember, of course, will depend on what we noticed at the time, i.e., on the information that we picked up, the schematic modification that took place. We cannot recall what we did not perceive, and we do not modify schemata unless they are actually used. Memory depends on attention, which is the subject of the next chapter.

Notes

1. Bartlett (1932, pp. 201–202).
2. Bartlett (1932, p. 201).
3. Noteworthy users of the term "schema" include Piaget (1952), Woodworth (1938), Kagan (1971), and Posner (1973[b]). A new and important systematic use is that of Rumelhart, Norman, and their associates at the University of California at San Diego (Bobrow and Norman, in press; Rumelhart 1975, in press; Rumelhart and Ortony, in press). Although Rumelhart's usage is directed at problems of memory and comprehension rather than perceiving—he deals with schemata for stories, as Bartlett did—it seems quite compatible with what I am proposing here. Moreover, it is commendably specific.
4. Miller, Galanter, and Pribram (1960). Another possibly helpful analogy is offered by Rumelhart (in press [a]): the relation between a schema and a particular instance of perceptual activity is somewhat like that between a play and a particular enactment of that play. Both this analogy and that of the programming format may also be misleading, however; schemata are more open and flexible than they suggest.
5. Neisser (1967).
6. Minsky (1975).
7. Goffman (1974).
8. Jenkins (1974).
9. Bronfenbrenner (1974).
10. Guzman (1968); Waltz (1975); Winograd (1972). Waltz's program is probably the most interesting of these for a perception psychologist because it takes ingenious advantage of constraints in the optical structure itself. Waltz noticed that the patterns of convexities, concavities, and shadows that real objects can present are sharply limited, and built knowledge of these restrictions into his program.
11. Perhaps the most important difference is that Minsky's frames are essentially static. He does not consider the effects of movement, or the temporal structuring of light

that movement produces. Moreover, he seems to think of frames as places to put information, rather than as plans for obtaining more of it. In addition, I believe that perceptual schemata disambiguate by *selecting* a particular alternative, not by adding more evidence for it as frames do. Finally, the notion of default assignment requires more careful analysis before it can be applied to human perception. In its present form, it would thoroughly confuse perception and mental imagery.

12. Shannon (1948); Broadbent (1958); Garner (1974).

13. In personal conversations, J. J. Gibson has expressed the opposite view. He thinks that his own conception of information cannot be reconciled with the traditional one.

14. Lindsay and Norman (1972); Posner (1973 [b]); Massaro (1975).

15. I am not trying to define any distinction between cognitive development and perceptual learning here. We do not know enough yet.

16. This idea has been suggested very often: e.g., by Broadbent (1966).

17. Wertheimer (1961).

18. The role of difference-nulling head movements in auditory localization is discussed by J. J. Gibson (1966); their relation to change in head size during development by Bower (1974).

19. Piaget (1952).

20. Price-Williams, D.R., Gordon, W., and Ramirez, W. (1969).

21. Turnbull (1961, p. 252).

22. Spelke (1976). I am indebted to Elizabeth Spelke for calling my attention to much of the literature on information seeking in infants.

23. Bower, Broughton, and Moore (1970[a], 1970[b]) used a stereoscopic shadow-caster to dangle illusory, intangible objects before their subjects. They reported that infants as young as seven days exhibited great surprise when their hands passed through the space occupied by the illusory image without contacting anything. This observation has not been easy to repeat, however, and it is somewhat

doubtful whether either reaching or stereoscopic depth perception develops early enough to make such behavior possible (Gordon and Yonas, in press).

24. Bower (1967, 1971, 1974).

25. That they do so in fact is demonstrated by some of Bower's earlier studies. Infants learned to make a response in the presence of a particular object, which was then shown in new positions or orientations. The babies always responded more to the same real object, even moved or turned, than to others that preserved such retinal features as projected size or projected shape (Bower, 1966).

26. Bower (1971, 1974).

27. Piaget (1954).

28. For a review of the literature from this point of view, see Harris (1975).

29. Piaget (1954).

30. Bower (1971, 1974).

31. Gibson (1966, p. 285; 1976).

32. Potter (1975).

33. Cohen (1970); Ball, Wood, and Smith (1975).

34. Brand (1971) and Ingling (1972) both showed that one can search for a number in general rather than just for particular numbers. My own studies of practiced visual search (Neisser, Novick, and Lazar, 1963) showed that even an arbitrary set of characters can eventually be incorporated in a single schema. These are highly specialized conditions, however, and subjects develop very sophisticated strategies to cope with them (Yonas and Pittenger, 1973; Neisser, 1974). Such strategies may have little generality. The categories defined by the task (i.e., the range of stimuli defined as targets) are "flat"; no members are central or prototypical. As Rosch (1973, 1975, in press) has shown, the categories of normal perception have a very different structure.

35. Jonides and Gleitman (1972).

36. See for example Pillsbury (1897); Bartlett (1932).

37. There have been many surveys of pattern recognition; e.g., Kolers (1968); Reed (1973).

Attention and the
Problem of Capacity

The information in any real situation is indefinitely rich. There is always more to see than anyone sees, and more to know than anyone knows. Why don't we see it?

The answer most frequently offered, theoretically seductive but quite misleading, is that we "filter it out." The seductive aspect of this suggestion is that, from a formal point of view, it is entirely correct. In mathematical information theory, a filter is any input-output device such that some of the information reaching the input has no effect on the output. Formally speaking, every human being filters out cosmic rays, insect pheromones, and every other kind of information that does not affect his behavior. Psychologically or biologically, however, this notion makes no sense. There is no mechanism, process, or system that functions to reject these stimuli such that they would be perceived if it were to fail. The perceiver simply does not pick them up, because he is not equipped to do so. The same principle applies even when he does have the sensory equipment to perceive something but merely lacks the skill; i.e., the necessary perceptual learning has not taken place. Selection is a positive process, not a negative one. Perceivers pick up only what they have schemata for, and willy-nilly ignore the rest.

The selectivity of perception is particularly interesting and significant in cases where the necessary schemata are present but go unused, and we overlook something on one occasion that could be easily perceived on another. We listen to what A is saying and ignore B, watch the defense rather than the offense in a football game, notice or fail to notice the pressure of ill-fitting shoes on our feet. These are instances of *selective attention,* a concept that has come to play a major role in modern psychology. Unfortunately, it is usually interpreted in ways that make the smallest possible concession to the facts of perceptual choice. As Kahneman puts it, ". . . the main function of the term 'attention' in post-behavioristic psychology is to provide a label for some of the internal mechanisms that determine the significance of stimuli and thereby make it impossible to predict behavior by stimulus considerations alone."[1] Recent years have witnessed an intensive search for these "internal mechanisms" at both the psychological and the physiological level. It is as if theorists were determined to divide the mind into two parts: a larger well-regulated portion whose activity depends on "stimulus considerations alone," and a small capricious mechanism in which choice is reluctantly permitted to exist. So far, the search has been in vain, and no separate mechanisms of attention have been found. In my opinion, that is because none exist.

The most interesting of the modern methods for studying attention is that of selective listening, devised by Cherry in the 1950s.[2] He made tape recordings of two independent spoken messages and played both to his subjects simultaneously, one at each ear and equally loud. He told them which message they were to attend (the "primary" one), and to make sure they did so he asked them to repeat it as it was presented, a procedure called *shadowing*. The subjects were able to do this easily, and almost entirely ignored the presence of the secondary message in doing so. Cherry's observations stimulated a host of ingenious experiments, that are of interest here for two reasons. First, the task itself is relatively familiar. We have all spent time in crowded rooms trying to follow one speaker rather than another, even if we have not demonstrated our attention by shadowing him. Second, it presents the subject with a more or less continuous and meaningful event over a substantial period of time. It is one of the few experimental procedures that offer information to perceivers in a natural way and allow the perceptual cycle to run its normal course.

Selective listening
and theories of attention

The two messages need not be presented to different ears; any distinction makes selective listening possible. They may come from different locations, or be spoken by two people with recognizably different voices, or just differ in loudness. It is easier to shadow meaningful material than nonsense, and it is possible (though difficult) to follow the primary message on the basis of meaning alone; i.e., when both messages were recorded by the same person and are played over a loudspeaker at equal volume.[3]

The decision to attend to one message rather than the other is a significant one, because it is an almost total commitment. Subjects know very little about the secondary message if they are asked about it afterwards; they cannot identify words that were repeated dozens of times and may not even know whether the message was in English. (They generally know whether the speaker was a man or a woman.) Under certain conditions, however, some of the secondary information is not entirely ignored. It became clear rather early that subjects occasionally noticed significant words on the secondary channel, especially their own names and repetitions or plausible continuations of the primary message.[4]

These findings led to a burst of theorizing about attention. Perhaps the most sophisticated theory was that of Treisman.[5] She suggested that only the attended message is processed for meaning, because a filtering mechanism attenuates the other information and prevents most of it from reaching higher brain centers. The filter was thought to detect physical features like voice quality and location (indeed, it must do so in order to select the right message) but does not know what anything means.

Beyond the filter, Treisman postulated an array of neural units (variously called *logogens, analyzing units, demons,* or *detectors*[6]) corresponding to words in the subject's vocabulary, which could be triggered by the information reaching them through the filter. Even the feeble filtered trickle from an unattended source might activate a logogen that was sufficiently primed and ready, like the one for the subject's own name or those for words made temporarily plausible by context. Conscious awareness was identified with activity at higher stages of the processing system: the activity of the logogens was assumed to be conscious, while that of the filter was not.

Treisman's theory is a particularly good example of the linear information processing model that was illustrated in Figure 1. The perceiver is regarded as a passive conduit for information, who happens to have a bottleneck early in his processing sequence. Most of the theories that have been put forward as alternatives to Treisman's share the same assumption; they simply locate the bottleneck at a different point. Deutsch and Deutsch,[7] for example, rejected the filter concept and assumed that everything is fully processed whether it is attended or not. On their hypothesis, selection occurs only at the stage of memory and action. Subjects in selective listening studies actually perceive both voices, but forget the unattended one so rapidly that it has little effect on their behavior or experience. In this version, therefore, the activity of the logogens is *not* conscious; we process information without being aware of it. Our mental machinery knows everything that is going on around us but discards most of it as unimportant before consciousness is reached.

To understand this increasingly popular view,[8] one must realize that it is based on a very sharp distinction between perception and memory. Any use of information a few milliseconds after it was presented, any anticipation, any use of environmental continuities—in short, any of the phenomena treated in this book—is regarded as dependent on memory rather than perception itself. Thus the Deutsches' claim that we "perceive" everything in our environment is not quite

as radical as it seems; it only means that we continuously register and then forget a lot of incoherent sensory
fragments.

Two lines of evidence have been adduced in favor of
the complete passive processing theory. One is based
on recent demonstrations of secondary pickup: it turns
out that more information is obtained from an "unattended" voice than the early experiments had
suggested. An interpretation of these demonstrations
will be offered later in this chapter. The other evidence
comes from certain new experiments on perceptual set.
These studies show, counterintuitively, that knowing
where (to what ear, in what sense modality, at what
place) a brief stimulus will be presented does not help
subjects to detect it.[9] Their findings will not be considered here, however, because they are just as irrelevant
to natural attention as traditional tachistoscopic research is to perception. We do not attend to ears, modalities, or points in the visual field, but to objects and
events; we do not do it in an instant but over time.

Selective looking

It seems to me that hypotheses like those of Treisman
or Deutsch and Deutsch are unnecessary. When perception is treated as something we do rather than as
something thrust upon us, no internal mechanisms of
selection are required at all. The listener follows a message by picking up the information that specifies it as a
separate event, and the information that specifies its
content and meaning. The more information he finds
available (contextual, spatial, etc.), the easier this task
becomes. Organisms are active: they do some things

and leave others undone. To pick one apple from a tree you need not filter out all the others; you just don't pick them. A theory of apple picking would have much to explain (How do you decide which one you want? Guide your hand to it? Grasp it?) but it would not have to specify a mechanism to keep unwanted apples out of your mouth.

One way to demonstrate that selection requires no special machinery would be to show that it occurs for every sort of perception, even where neither practice nor evolution is likely to have provided a selective mechanism. To this end, Robert Becklen and I devised a visual analogue of the selective listening paradigm.[10] We videotaped two kinds of "games," and then used a mirror to show them in full visual overlap, rather as if a television set were somehow showing two channels at once (see Figure 3). Subjects were asked to attend to one of the games and ignore the other, pressing a response key at every occurrence of certain target events (e.g., throws of the ball) in the attended game. The results were clear. At an event rate of about 40 targets per minute, it was nearly as easy to follow one game when it was superimposed on another as when it was shown by itself. The error rate was only about three percent, and subjects had no difficulty even on the first trial. We have since established that this ability does not depend on following the attended game with one's eyes, and that it undergoes little change even when the two games are visually similar.[11] Performance deteriorates only when subjects must monitor both games at once; this task produces many complaints and high error rates.

Just as one can shadow a primary message in the presence of a irrelevant voice, so one can follow a vi-

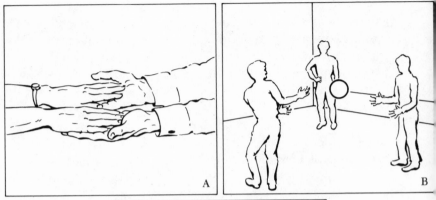

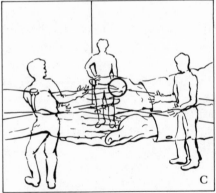

FIGURE 3. *The selective looking experiment.* [From Selective
looking: attending to visually-specified events, by U.
Neisser and R. Becklen. *Cognitive Psychology,*
7(1975):480–494.]

sually given primary event and ignore another equally
present to the eyes. The naturalness of this task and the
lack of interference from the other episode are remarkable. One does not *see* the irrelevant game, just as one
does not hear the unattended message in a selective
listening task, although one has a sense that something
else is there. How is this possible? We can hardly be

equipped with a special filtering mechanism to eliminate unwanted visually overlapping episodes; they
rarely occur in ordinary life. In any case, how could
such a mechanism work? The primary and secondary
events are not distinguished by location or modality but
by their intrinsic structures alone.

The cyclic model of perception makes it easy to
understand these results. Only the attended episode is
involved in the cycle of anticipations, explorations, and
information pickup; therefore, only it is seen. Attention
is nothing but perception: we choose what we will see
by anticipating the structured information it will
provide.

The same principles apply to selective listening. We
choose what we will hear by actively engaging ourselves with it, not by shutting out its competitors. (This
view is confirmed—or at least not contradicted—by recent work in sensory neurophysiology. Shifts of attention are not reflected in quantitative reductions of the
inflow along certain nerves, as was once supposed, but
by very general changes in cerebral activity.[12]) What,
then, happens to unattended information? In general,
nothing happens to it. It suffers the fate of the many
kinds of information for which we have no schemata at
all: we simply don't pick it up. But why not? Would it
not be to our advantage to do so? Is it impossible to
deploy more than one schema at a time? The answer to
this question, interestingly enough, depends not on
general psychological principles but on the sophistication of the subject.

Dual attention as an acquired skill

Contemporary theories of attention have another
common characteristic. Not only do they treat the mind

as a passive mechanism, but they assume that the mechanism is fixed. The theories make no distinctions between skilled and unskilled subjects, between those who are trying to pick up information from the secondary message and those who only want to ignore it, or between adults and children. It is not even easy to see how such distinctions could be introduced into the complete passive processing theory; if a mechanism processed everything anyway, there would be little room for improvement. In Treisman's theory one might assume that the filter becomes more efficient with age or experience, but then sophisticated subjects should pick up *less* information than naive ones. Some psychologists have actually advocated this curious doctrine, and have carried out developmental studies of attention in the hope of finding poorer performance at older ages. In my judgment, their efforts have met with little success.[13]

What happens when people deliberately try to pick up information from a secondary message? Several experimenters have embedded target numerals in prose passages (As for example in seven this sentence) and have asked subjects to give a signal or to stop shadowing when they detected one. Unpracticed subjects rarely notice such targets. Moreover, the few secondary detections that do occur are apparently independent of context. A subject listening for numerals is as likely to resond to *for* in "there was little reason for his action" as to *four* in "the leaves were a brilliant four green" in a message to which he is not attending, though he would rarely make such a mistake on the primary text.[14] As Treisman points out,[15] these results argue strongly against the notion that all inputs are analyzed. If they were, why wouldn't subjects detect targets equally well in either message? Apparently they are not picking up the information they need from the secondary one. Filter theory would say that this is because they have been able to block it out, while the active theory proposed here suggests that they can't manage to pick it up in the first place. If the latter view is correct, such subjects lack a skill which they might potentially acquire. At least one bit of data indicates that this is true. After practicing a dual shadowing and number-detecting task for several hours, Neville Moray[16] improved his own detection rate in the secondary channel to 83 percent in a task where naive subjects average 4 percent. His ability may not have been the result of the experimental practice alone; Moray is a psychologist who has worked extensively with shadowing experiments. It is clear, however, that we should not generalize carelessly from average results obtained with naive subjects to statements about human perceptual mechanisms.

This experiment raises questions that are far older than the filter theory of attention. Did Moray really attend to both messages at once? Indeed, it is possible to attend to two things at once? Or can secondary tasks be carried out only "automatically," "outside of consciousness"? If so, what are the limits of automatic, mental activity? As we shall see, the evidence on these matters suggests that human cognitive activity would be more usefully conceived as a collection of acquired skills than as the operation of a single fixed mechanism.

Experiments on doing two things at once date back to the nineteenth century. The most interesting of them, because it involved extended practice, was conducted by Gertrude Stein and Leon M. Solomons at Harvard.[17] They tried to teach themselves to read and write at the same time, an achievement that they termed "automatic writing." They practiced themselves at a series of progressively more difficult tasks: reading while moving a planchette, reading while writing dictated words, reading while writing spontaneously, and reading one story aloud while copying down another at dictation. They intended to, and did, practice each of these tasks until one of the activities became automatic, i.e., was no longer conscious. Unfortunately, their only interest was in this introspectively defined issue, so they reported no data on amount of practice or reading speed.

Part of the Solomons and Stein study was replicated in 1915 by Downey and Anderson,[18] who also copied dictated words while they read silently. They achieved marked improvements in reading rate after seventeen hours of practice, but failed to reach the speed with which they read under normal conditions. Unlike Solomons and Stein, Downey and Anderson never achieved "automatism": they remained aware of the words they were copying. This inconsistency is not surprising, I think; introspective reports of such matters are notoriously unreliable.

Recently, Elizabeth Spelke and William Hirst have carried out a replication and extension of the Solomons and Stein experiment at Cornell.[19] They made an important break with tradition by not using themselves as the only subjects; two college students worked in the experiment an hour a day for an entire semester. The subjects read stories silently while copying words that the experimenter dictated one after the other (each word was presented as soon as the preceding one had been copied). At first they found the dual task difficult, as one might expect, and read much more slowly than under normal conditions. After about six weeks of practice, however, their reading speeds had returned to

normal. Careful tests showed that they were also reading with full comprehension.

During this phase of the experiment, the dictated
words had been chosen at random. Would the subjects
notice departures from randomness? Sublists were introduced in the eighth week: 20 consecutive words
from a particular category, 20 plural nouns, 20 words
that consisted of a series of meaningful sentences. Each
type of structured sublist was presented several times,
but neither subject commented on any of them. (They
would surely have remarked on these patterns if they
had observed them, because when a sublist of 20 *rhym-
ing* words was presented at the end of the week they
noticed it immediately, with some amusement.) When
the sublists were later shown to them, it was not easy to
convince the subjects of what had actually happened.
Had they really copied, say, "trolley, skates, truck,
horse, airplane, tractor, car, rocket, bike, taxi, scooter,
jet, trailer, subway, tank, feet, cab, ship, tricycle, van"
without noticing the category? They had.

The fact that people do not notice something is no
evidence that they could not have noticed it if they had
tried. In the next phase of the experiment, therefore, the
subjects were told that (unspecified) categories and sentences would occasionally be embedded among the
dictated words, and they were asked to report such
occurrences. The additional task caused some decre-
ment in their reading performance at first—one subject
slowed down and the other read with decreased comprehension—but they eventually recovered; on many
trials they detected virtually all the categories and most
of the sentences while reading normally. Finally, they
were asked to categorize each dictated word as it was
spoken, i.e., to write down the category from which it

was drawn instead of the word itself. After a good deal of additional practice, this too could be combined with reading at normal speed and comprehension.

The subjects of the Spelke-Hirst experiment were obviously attending to the dictated words as well as to the story, and not simply in an automatic way. Their performance cannot be explained by conventional theories of attention. It seems clear that the amount of information picked up from one source while attending to another is not limited by any fixed mechanisms at all, and therefore *no* specific hypothesis about such mechanisms can be correct. Instead, performance depends on the skill of the observer. Practiced subjects can do what seems impossible to the novice as well as to the theorist.

In retrospect, perhaps we should not have been surprised by this result. Equally dramatic improvements occur in more mundane skills. When one first learns to drive, for example, control of the car requires one's full attention. Later, the practiced driver can shift gears and turn corners and overtake trucks while arguing vigorously about (say) psychological theory. Many skilled typists can carry on a conversation while typing from copy, but it seems unlikely that they could do so without practice; certainly I can't. Most adults can talk or think while putting on their overcoats or tying their shoes, but young children cannot; the wise parent does not converse with his or her six-year-old while the latter is getting dressed for school.

Although apparently no modern psychologists besides Hirst and Spelke have examined the development of such multiple skills, several studies of individuals who had already achieved a high degree of proficiency confirm their findings. Skilled pianists can shadow

prose while sight-reading music at the piano,[20] and professional typists can type from copy while shadowing or
while reciting nursery rhymes from memory.[21] The
pickup of information from secondary sources does not
occur automatically, but neither is it prevented by any
filtering mechanism. The more skilled the perceiver,
the more he can perceive.

Automatic pickup?

This principle has implications even for experiments
with unpracticed subjects. No adult is entirely naive in
dealing with multiple sources of information. Everyone
has had some kind of relevant experience—trying to
listen to the radio and study at the same time, attending
to what a lecturer is saying while noting down what he
said before, being trapped in a boring conversation and
trying to overhear a neighboring one that is more interesting. It is not easy to specify these skills, nor to
define their relevance to any given experiment, but we
should not be surprised to find an occasional demonstration of their effects.

There have been several recent demonstrations of
this kind. They are all based on indirect measures of the
influence of "unattended" information, because asking
subjects about it explicitly yields such negative results.
The rapidity with which subjects make their shadowing
responses to the primary message, for example, can be
influenced by a related word in the secondary one.[22]
The effect is subtle, however; it works differently for
synonyms and antonyms in ways that vary from one laboratory to another, and it may be restricted to the early
portions of stimulus lists.[23] Similarly, several studies

have shown that a person's interpretation of an ambiguous sentence in the primary message can be biased by concurrently presented secondary information, but in one experiment the effect could be obtained only with M.I.T. students and not with subjects from Harvard.[24] The most impressive of these demonstrations is that of Corteen and Wood,[25] who first sensitized their subjects to certain words by associating them with electric shock. When those words (or related ones) were subsequently included in a secondary message during selective listening, they triggered physiological responses indicative of alarm. There have been both failures and successes among the attempts to replicate this study.[26]

In stressing that these findings are difficult to replicate, I do not mean to deny that they are genuine. There is now no doubt that some "naive" subjects pick up the meanings of some "irrelevant" words, at least under some conditions. It has been suggested that this fact invalidates the filter theory, and it probably does. We need not conclude, however, that *all* subjects pick up *all* meanings of *all* irrelevant words, and it would be a mistake to theorize about attention as if this had been demonstrated. The results of the experiments are better ascribed to the intermittent exercise of casually acquired skills than to the operation of automatic mechanisms.

I do not mean to deny the existence of automatic mechanisms altogether. Information pickup is not entirely under voluntary control; we would be too absentminded to survive if it were. Loud noises, rhythmic repetitions of stimuli, sudden visible movements, and painful stimuli are examples of signals that we are always ready for. Infants are surely born with schemata to accept such information, which is used to begin new cycles of perceptual activity. Although everyone soon develops more complex schemata to extract subtler kinds of information from his environment, the simpler ones retain a measure of autonomy. Such schemata operate outside of attention—that is, they are continually ready to detect their proper signals no matter what other perceptual cycle may be in progress—and they are more or less indifferent to context and meaning. I once suggested that they be called *preattentive processes.*[27] The term is still serviceable, but it should not be overused. Although our ability to pick up information outside the mainstream of ongoing activity is sometimes based on automatic systems of this kind, it can also be the result of acquired skill and deliberate choice. One of the results obtained by Spelke and Hirst can serve to illustrate this difference. Their subjects noticed spontaneously that a series of successively dictated words all rhymed; only after being forewarned did they notice instances of common category membership.

There are also occasions when other kinds of signals seem to compel our attention. It is widely assumed that people can be conditioned to perceive and respond to certain stimuli whether they want to or not, regardless of their set or attitude of the moment. Such phenomena are often demonstrated with isolated verbal stimuli. In the *Stroop Test,* for example, subjects must name the colors of the inks in which words are printed and ignore the words themselves.[28] This is not easy to do; it becomes excruciatingly difficult if the words are actually color names, so that the correct response to the word *yellow* is "blue" when it happens to be printed in blue ink. Nevertheless, this finding should be interpreted cautiously. The color names do not really force themselves on the subject willy-nilly. The instructions *re-quire* that he be prepared to utter color names, so the relevant schemata are far from dormant or passive. He is really in a kind of double bind: he must be ready to say "yellow" as fast as possible, but must refrain from saying it when its most adequate stimulus appears. If the double bind is lifted by the introduction of a different response requirement—if he is allowed to push a button corresponding to the ink color instead of naming it—the difficulty is greatly reduced.[29]

There are many similar effects. When a numeral is flashed on a screen as another is spoken, a subject told to repeat the former (verbally) has difficulty in ignoring the latter.[30] This does not mean heard numerals cannot be ignored (subjects in selective listening studies find it difficult even to detect them), but rather that asking someone to detect and ignore them in the same instant puts an unaccustomed burden on his natural skills.

The fact that subjects can perform such tasks at all requires some comment. They do so by deliberately ignoring information that would normally govern their behavior. Are they filtering it out? I would prefer to say that they refrain from picking it up even though they could do so if they wished. This may not be easy when a long-practiced skill is involved: self-restraint in such cases is notoriously difficult. Nevertheless, its achievement does not call for the creation of a new barrier, but for the abandonment of an old activity.

The possibility of automatic behavioral control has been greatly exaggerated by both psychologists and laymen. Even the "conditioning" of simple autonomic responses is generally influenced by context and intent. Subjects who are given an electric shock every time a certain word appears soon develop a strong galvanic skin response to its presentation, but the response disappears or is greatly modified as soon as the shock electrodes are removed.[31] (Methods of "lie detection" based on autonomic responses are generally quite unreliable.[32]) Other kinds of conditioning are equally labile, and frequently fail to generalize to new situations. I doubt that any responses other than the primitive preattentive ones ever become genuinely automatic, in the sense that they can be elicited independently of the situation and the subject's own plans and purposes.

This should not be taken to imply that we always know what we are doing or why we are doing it. We are very often unaware of the real reasons for our actions; they are "unconscious," as Freud put it. But our inability to give a good account of our own behavior does not mean that we are being automatically controlled by simple stimuli; it means that we do not attend to the same information when we describe our behavior as when we execute it. The entire notion of behavioral control is based on an inadequate conception of human nature and cognitive activity. This issue will be considered more carefully in Chapter 9.

The limits of capacity

It is often argued that there must be an overall limit to a person's capacity for information. Acceptance of this assumption frequently goes along with some form of filter theory: a special mechanism is postulated to protect the limited capacity from overload. Arguments of this kind are common not only in experimental psychology but in neighboring disciplines. They have led neurophysiologists to look for filtering mechanisms in the nervous system, and sociologists to bewail the information overload that burdens the inhabitants of modern society. We have seen, however, that such filters are not needed and probably do not exist. In my opinion, the notion of a single central information limit is equally misguided. Human abilities do have limitations, but they are not so monolithic or quantitative as such a notion would suggest. The very concept of "capacity" seems better suited to a passive vessel into which things are put than to an active and developing structure.

The belief in a fixed cognitive capacity has been so widely accepted that it deserves very careful examination. It has several roots. One of them is closely related to the concept of consciousness, and will be considered in a later section of this chapter. Another, which can be quickly dismissed, is based on what appears to be a logical and a priori argument. According to a theorem in the mathematical theory of communication, when the rate of information input to any finite channel exceeds a certain value (called the channel's capacity) not all of it can be transmitted without error. Because the brain itself is finite and because it transmits information, this theorem has been taken as proof that there must be a limit to human capacity as well.

While such an argument is valid in principle, it is of dubious relevance to psychology. The brain contains millions of neurons, in unimaginably subtle relationships with one another. Who can say how high the limit imposed by such a "mechanism" may be? No one has ever demonstrated that the facts of selective attention have any relation to the brain's real capacity, if it has one at all. Indeed, no psychological fact has anything to do with the overall size of the brain. Contrary to popular assumption, we have no great cerebral storehouse that is in danger of becoming overcrowded. There are probably no quantitative limits on long-term memory, for example; you can go on meeting new people, acquiring new languages, and exploring new environments as long as your inclinations and energy last. Similarly, there is no physiologically or mathematically established limit on how much information we can pick up at once.

At another pole from this abstract argument, and more worthy of detailed consideration, are the limitations that seem to reveal themselves in everyday life. Everyone knows that we become inefficient if we attempt too much; trying to do several things at once often ends in failure to do any of them adequately. These observations are surely valid, but there is no reason why they should all be explained by an overload in some central piece of machinery. It is equally possible that the limiting factors are specific to the combinations of individual activities and skills involved. Consider our physical abilities: they are obviously finite, but their limitations do not arise from any single source. The limit on how fast we can run is not based on the same factors as the maximum weight we can lift; the sharpness of our visual acuity is not constrained by whatever sets the minimum oculomotor reaction time. Why should a single mechanism be held responsible for all our cognitive limitations?

Several sources of difficulty can arise when people try to do two things at once. (The fact that such difficulties can often be eliminated by practice does not make them unimportant. If we understood them, we might be able to distinguish the cases that will yield to practice from those that will not.) First, the two tasks may simply require some part of the body to execute incompatible movements, like writing and throwing a ball with the same hand. Less obviously, they may *seem* to require incompatible movements, like writing with one hand and throwing a ball with the other. These two acts involve posture and muscular timing in the entire body as well as movements of the arm, and since they are learned separately they will generally be based on incompatible timings and postures. It is probably possible to do them together, but only by first reorganizing each one in a fundamental way.

A similar difficulty arises when we try to use the same perceptual schemata for two incompatible purposes at once. We cannot simultaneously imagine one spatial arrangement of objects and observe another, for example (see Chapter 7). Similarly, we cannot rehearse two rhythmic patterns of digits simultaneously. (For this purpose, the memory span may be regarded as a detailed anticipation of temporally structured acoustic information.) If a subject attempts something like this in a dual-listening experiment, switching back and forth between two messages and trying to remember each one as if it were a meaningless string, his performance will reflect that limitation. It would be a mistake to treat this as the fundamental reason for the difficulty of the double task, however. It only represents the inefficiency of one particular and somewhat awkward strategy.

Another kind of conflict appears when the critical signals for one task are actually masked by concurrent stimuli in the other. For example, one voice in a dual listening study may be so loud that it drowns the other out. In this case there is no question of a cognitive limitation at all; the information needed for one of the tasks is simply no longer available. If the masking is only partial, however, practice may still result in improved performance. The subject can learn what kinds of information are least effectively masked, and can come to rely on them more heavily than he would under normal conditions.

One reason for doubting the existence of a single central capacity is that so many pairs of continuous and time-dependent activities *can* be successfully combined by practiced subjects: driving and talking, for example, or shadowing and sight-reading music. It has often been observed, however, that such combinations tend to break down when either task becomes unexpectedly difficult. Drivers stop talking when an emergency situation looms up, and the pianist may stop shadowing when he must play a particularly complex passage. Such observations could indeed be attributed to a central mechanism that was being shared by both tasks, and is suddenly overloaded. This hypothesis is not the only possible one, however. Emergency situations are almost invariably unfamiliar and require relatively unpracticed applications of driving or piano-playing skill. In general, the subject will not yet have learned how to combine that particular application with the secondary task, and his performance would necessarily suffer as a result. It is to avoid this degradation of performance that he temporarily interrupts one of the tasks. If he is practiced enough to have encountered that sort of emergency often before, no interruption is necessary.

In short, difficulties are bound to arise whenever we begin to combine two tasks that have no natural relationship to each other. There are usually many ways to do any given thing, and the pattern of skills acquired separately for task A will be rarely be optimal for combining it with task B. We do not often find ourselves in contrived dual-task situations, and hence we do not learn our basic skills in their most combinable forms.

The kinds of difficulty mentioned above do not account for all the problems we encounter when we try to do two things at once. One particularly important case concerns the perception of two meaningful and continuous events in the same modality. It is excruciatingly difficult to follow both games at once in the selective looking experiment or to attend to a pair of meaningful and interesting conversations. The work of Spelke and Hirst indicates that practice can produce dramatic improvements in dual tasks, but even their subjects were not asked to extract contextually given meaning from the dictated secondary message. Perhaps even this would eventually become possible, but also perhaps not. Even if it is possible, the question of why it is so difficult would still remain.

The problem is surely not one of overall "information load." Following two different messages, even when they are simple in content, seems to be much harder than understanding a single message of whatever complexity. It would be even more unsatisfactory, however, to explain the difficulty by postulating some speech center in the brain that can only handle one signal at a time. Such a postulate would merely lead to a restatement of the problem: why can't the speech center follow two messages at once?

It is possible that we never learn to handle dual tasks only because we rarely have any serious occasion to try. We listen to conversations primarily so we can participate in them, or at least imagine doing so, and this is only possible with one message at a time. I am skeptical of this hypothesis, however; if dual listening were really feasible someone would surely have discovered and made use of it already. It seems more likely that there is some genuine informational impediment to the parallel development of independent but similar schemata. If each schema involves anticipations that span appreciable amounts of time, for example, (as is necessarily the case in meaningful listening, reading, or looking) the problem of applying new information to the correct schema may be insuperable. Further research may clarify this question.

Consciousness

One final argument for the notion of a limited processing capacity remains to be considered. It is often said that a person can only be *conscious* of one thing at a time. This has suggested that there is a crucial mechanism of fixed size somewhere in the head that is mysteriously and directly observable. Our introspectively given experience would then be limited to the contents of that decisive vessel, and all other aspects of processing would remain subconscious or unconscious.

This is an old idea. Psychologists at least since Freud have been quite ready to treat consciousness as a piece of the mind or a place in the head. (It is surprising how contemporary Freud's theory is. *The Interpretation of Dreams* even includes flow charts on which the locations of Conscious, Unconscious, and Preconscious are clearly marked.[33]) It is currently a very popular notion, and with good reason. It represents a theoretical coup: not only are the facts of attention apparently explained, but psychology's most elusive target is finally nailed down to a box in a flow chart.

We have already considered the shortcomings of such a view as a theory of attention. It is also inadequate as an introspective account of immediate phenomenal ex-

perience. Introspection does *not* necessarily show that
one is aware of only a single thing at a time. I think that
people report the singleness of consciousness largely
because the philosophical assumptions of our culture
require it; everyone has learned how to reconcile those
assumptions with his mental life and to overlook what
does not fit. What we report about private experience
depends very heavily on what Orne has called the
"demand characteristics" of the situation.[34] The frequency with which early twentieth-century psychologists reported mental imagery, for example, depended
on the laboratory in which they were working; the vividness that contemporary subjects assign to their images
can be markedly increased by asking them the right sort
of question.[35] The introspections offered by the subjects
of Spelke and Hirst were chaotic and inconsistent:
sometimes they knew exactly what they were writing,
sometimes they were not aware of having written at all.
The very notion of "a single thing" is far from clear:
how many things am I aware of when I listen to an
orchestra, watch a ballet, drive a car, make love?

The treatment of consciousness as a processing stage
is unsatisfactory in a still more fundamental way. It does
justice neither to the usages of the word *consciousness*
in ordinary discourse nor to the subtleties of experience. A better conception of consciousness, which has
been suggested many times in the history of psychology, would recognize it as an aspect of activity rather
than as an independently definable mechanism. Consciousness undergoes changes throughout the course of
life because we learn to pick up new sorts of information in new ways. These processes of change are called
cognitive development in some contexts and perceptual
learning in others; in political situations they have re-

cently been called consciousness raising. We are conscious *of* objects, events, and situations.

It is true, of course, that not everything of which we are conscious exists in the environment. We have thoughts, images, and feelings as well that may or may not be accessible to introspective report. In particular, our anticipatory schemata seem to have an inner aspect; we are aware of them. Later chapters will consider what this might mean and how we manage to report on it, but no theory of consciousness will be presented anywhere in this book. Such theories degenerate too easily into misleading accounts of limited-capacity devices. Consciousness is an aspect of mental activity, not a switching center on the intrapsychic railway.

Notes

1. Kahneman (1973, p. 2).
2. Cherry (1953); Cherry and Taylor (1954).
3. See Neisser (1967) for references to this work.
4. Moray (1959); Treisman (1964[b], 1969).
5. Treisman (1964 [b], 1969).
6. The term *logogen* is due to Morton (1969); *demon* was coined by Selfridge (1959), whose theory was the first of this kind. The currently popular term is *detector*.
7. Deutsch and Deutsch (1963). See also the interchange between Treisman and Geffen (1967) and Deutsch, Deutsch, and Lindsay (1967).
8. E.g., Shiffrin (in press); Posner and Synder (1975).
9. Shiffrin and Gardner (1972); Shiffrin and Grantham (1974); Shiffrin, Pisoni, and Castaneda-Mendez (1974).
10. Neisser and Becklen (1975). The original impetus for our work was a demonstration reported by Kolers (1969, 1972).

11. The study of selective looking under fixation conditions is that of Littman and Becklen (in press). A more recent study involving the superimposition of two more or less similar ball games has been completed but is not yet fully analyzed.

12. Hernandez-Peon and his colleagues (1956) originally reported that the afferent signals in the cat's auditory nerve produced by a train of clicks were reduced when the cat became interested in a visible mouse. Worden (1966), however, has shown that this result was artifactual. Picton, Hillyard, Galambos, and Schiff (1971) found no change in human auditory-nerve activity as a result of shifts of attention, and their findings have been repeatedly corroborated. A recent review by Hillyard and Picton (in press) shows that selective attention is accompanied by a wide variety of changes in cerebral evoked potentials, but these changes are compatible with many theoretical interpretations.

13. Maccoby and Hagen (1965), Hagen (1967), Siegel and Stevenson (1966), Hawkins (1973).

14. Treisman and Geffen (1967); Treisman and Riley (1969); Glucksberg and Cowen (1970); Klapp and Lee (1974).

15. Treisman and Geffen (1967).

16. Underwood (1974).

17. Solomons and Stein (1896).

18. Downey and Anderson (1915).

19. Spelke, Hirst, and Neisser (1976).

20. Allport, Antonis, and Reynolds (1972).

21. Shaffer (1975).

22. Lewis (1970).

23. Bryden (1972); Treisman, Squire, and Green (1974).

24. The M.I.T./Harvard study is that of Lackner and Garrett (1972); see also Mackay (1973).

25. Corteen and Wood (1972).

26. There have been one unsuccessful as well as two successful replications of this effect in Corteen's laboratory. (See Corteen and Dunn [1974]. I am indebted to Dr. Corteen

for a very helpful personal communication on this matter.)
A similar effect was briefly reported earlier by Moray
(1970). On the other hand, at least two other attempts to
demonstrate the phenomenon have not succeeded
(Wardlaw and Kroll, in press; Bowers, 1976). See also von
Wright, Anderson, and Stenman (1975).

27. Neisser (1967). The definition of *preattentive* offered
there was wider than the one I am now suggesting.

28. Stroop (1935); Jensen and Rohwer (1966); Dyer (1973).

29. Pritchatt (1968).

30. Greenwald (1970).

31. Mandel and Bridger (1973).

32. Lykken (1974).

33. Freud (1900).

34. Orne (1962).

35. The effects of demand characteristics on the vividness of
imagery appeared in a study conducted by Peter Sheehan
and myself (Sheehan and Neisser, 1969). I have discussed
this problem in slightly more detail elsewhere (Neisser,
1972).

Cognitive Maps

People move. They turn their heads, shift their bodies, walk to the next room, go to the store, or travel around the world. The nature of perception cannot be understood without taking their mobility into account. Each of our perceptual systems[1] has evolved to take advantage of the special kinds of information that motion makes available. Perceiving is often most effective during motion: we localize sounds with maximum accuracy if we move our heads while we listen and feel the shapes of objects especially well if we explore them actively with our hands. The case of vision is particularly important, and easily misunderstood. Motion changes some, but not necessarily all, of the available optical information: our eyes can partially compensate for head motion by moving in their sockets to maintain fixation on a target object. This kind of compensation is important because it offers prolonged detail vision of things that would otherwise slide quickly out of sight. Nevertheless, it must not be taken to imply that visual perception requires an unchanging retinal image in the way that photography requires a stable optical image on the film of a camera. Compensating movements only determine what is to be foveal; they cannot prevent the retinal image as a whole from changing substantially. These ubiquitous changes should not be thought of as mere nuisances or sources of blur; they provide invaluable information about the layout of the environment and the movement of the observer himself within it. Moreover, the information produced by more extensive movements—by locomotion—is fundamental to spatial orientation in the larger sense. In short, the motionless observer with a fixed head who serves as the subject in so many perception experiments is in an unusual and remarkably unfavorable situation. The motion-produced information that he lacks is crucial for normal vision.[2]

Motion changes the available stimulus information in many ways. Even a shift of the head sideways is enough to reveal new aspects of most nearby objects and to occlude others that were visible before. The patterns of occlusion and disocclusion[3] produced in this way specify the relative positions of both the observer and the objects themselves. More extensive movements have more dramatic visual consequences. When we go around a corner or through a door, we obtain whole new vistas that were previously hidden.[4] This means that evey opaque object—indeed, every occluding edge—defines a region that could be brought into view by some movement. In this way, the normal environment always includes perceptually specified potential locations for things yet unseen. Schemata incorporate this fact. What the perceiver will see when he has moved stands in an already defined relation ("behind") to what is presently visible. The relative positions of objects are known before specific information about them becomes available to the eye. Information picked up as a result of ego-motion is thus systematically related to existing schemata, and in particular to a cognitive map or orienting schema of the nearby environment.

Cognitive maps as schemata

The term *cognitive map* was coined long ago by Tolman.[5] It has gained new currency in the last few years, as psychologists, geographers, planners, and other professionals have become increasingly interested in problems of spatial orientation.[6] Their interest is natural; spatial schemata have a powerful hold over our imaginations. To a remarkable extent, they *are* our imaginations. Spatial organization generates a wonderful variety of metaphors for the mind: we are "in a position" to know something, have knowledge that is "wide" or "deep," look at "the other side" of a question, study "areas" and "fields" of learning. A person who does not have an adequate orienting schema is "lost"—a distressing situation with its own array of metaphorical extensions.[7]

Cognitive maps are often discussed as if they were mental pictures of the environment that could be examined at leisure by the mind's eye while the mind's owner reclined in his armchair. That interpretation shines through the passage with which Kenneth Boulding begins his book *The Image:*

As I sit at my desk, I know where I am. I see before me a window; beyond that some trees; beyond that the red roofs of the campus of Stanford University; beyond them the trees and rooftops which mark the town of Palo Alto; beyond them the bare golden hills of the Hamilton Range. I know, however, more than I can see. Behind me, although I am not looking in that direction, I know there is a window, and beyond that the little campus of the Center for Advanced Study in the Behavioral Sciences; beyond that the Coast Range; beyond that the Pacific Ocean. Looking ahead of me again, I know that beyond the mountains that close my present horizon, there is a broad valley; beyond that a still higher range of mountains; beyond that other mountains, range upon range, until we come to the Rockies; beyond that the Great Plains and the Mississippi; beyond that the Alleghenies; beyond that the Eastern seaboard; beyond that the Atlantic Ocean . . .[8]

There can be no doubt that Boulding has used a cognitive map as the basis for these remarks. Nevertheless, it may be unwise to define cognitive maps by the ability to give such descriptions or to have such images. I will attempt the opposite here, and frequently use the term "orienting schema" as a synonym for "cognitive map" to emphasize that it is an active, information-seeking structure. Instead of defining a cognitive map as a kind of image, I will propose (in Chapter 7) that spatial imagery itself is just an aspect of the functioning of orienting schemata. Like other schemata, they accept information and direct action. Just as I have an object schema that accepts information about my desk lamp and directs further exploration of it, I also have a cognitive map of my whole office and its setting to accept information about the office and to direct my movements within it. The lamp schema is a part of the larger orienting schema, just as the lamp itself is a part of the real environment. The perceptual cycle that was diagrammed in Figure 2 is embedded in a more inclusive cycle of exploration and information pickup that covers more ground and takes more time. Figure 4 illustrates this relationship.

Cognitive psychologists have often assumed that mental activity flows internally from the specific to the general, from details of the input pattern to categories

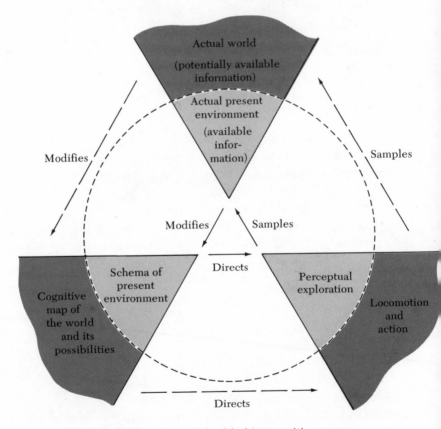

FIGURE 4. *Schemata as embedded in cognitive maps.*

and abstractions. There are said to be successive *stages*, or *levels* of processing.[9] It is assumed that in seeing a printed word, for example, we first determine the graphic features of the individual letters, then identify the letters, then identify the word itself, realize its meaning, and finally perhaps assign it to a particular category or semantic type. The example of schema and cognitive map suggests a rather different model of the relation between activities of different orders. They are *embedded* rather than successive. Their relationship parallels that of the real objects with which they deal. Just as the room and the lamp exist together, one including the other, so my orienting schema and my schema of the lamp are simultaneously active, the former including the latter. Each is a phase of a cyclic interaction with the environment; both interactions occur continuously. They cannot be comfortably separated. I could view the lamp without a surrounding room, but my perception will always be guided by some general cognitive map as well as by a specific perceptual schema. The room might lack a lamp, but there would always be some object or space between objects in the part of the room where it used to be. Ordinary perception relies heavily on the mutual support of these different levels of interaction with the environment.[10] So does behavior, for that matter. Actions are hierarchically embedded in more extensive actions and are motivated by anticipated consequences at various levels of schematic organization.[11]

Movement-produced information

Orienting schemata are not just assemblages of object schemata. They include information about the spatial

relations between objects, about their positions in the
environment. Although some information about spatial
arrangement can be picked up by even a stationary observer, much more becomes available if he begins to
move. The act of locomotion, which *requires* more information if it is to be carried out successfully, also *produces* more information for the moving perceiver. If this
were not so, it is unlikely that moving animals would
have evolved.

The organism in motion has access to two special
kinds of optical information. One of these is *parallax,*
based on the difference between the optic arrays at
separate station points. A shift of the eye from one position to another generally produces a new stimulus
pattern, and the discrepancies between successive
patterns can specify the shapes, positions, and layouts
of visible objects. It is also possible to obtain this sort of
information without actually moving. Human beings
and a few other animals can use *binocular* parallax as an
effective substitute. Because our two eyes are at different positions in our heads, most arrangements of objects
produce slightly discrepant patterns on the two retinae.
This discrepancy is a depth cue; i.e., it specifies the real
shapes and layout of the objects. (The stereoscope is a
device for counterfeiting such information to produce
illusory depth.) In a sense, binocular vision is an ingenious evolutionary trick for getting the advantages of
motion parallax without actually moving.

Motion of the observer also provides a second and
more important kind of information, which cannot be
simulated stereoscopically. Since movement is a continuous process, it creates continuous changes—flow
patterns—in the optical structure available to the eye.
Not only do different faces of objects come into view as

the perceiver moves, but the optically projected shapes of these faces undergo systematic changes. (It would be a mistake to describe the changes as "distortions" of shape. The point is not that one momentary retinal projection is accurate while the others are distorted, but that the optical transformations produced by movement specify the real layout of the environment.) Similarly, the retinal length and orientation of nearly every visible edge vary continuously during motion. It was noted earlier that kinetic information of this kind becomes available whenever a nearby object moves. The point here is that motion of the observer is equally or more informative.

The observer's movement does not provide information only about the environment. The pattern of change and invariance available to his eyes specifies his own movements as well. As he moves forward, for example, the retinal projections of every visible surface in the forward half of the environment become steadily larger. Under normal conditions, no purely environmental change can create this particular optical flow. It specifies ego motion and nothing else. Moreover, the manner in which the projections grow larger is not arbitrary: every projected point except one moves steadily outward. The single exception is the very point toward which the perceiver is moving. Thus not only the fact that he is moving but the direction of his motion is fully specified.[12]

The availability of this kind of optical structure means that one can see one's own position and one's own movement as well as the layout of the environment. Such perception is not indirect or inferential; information about oneself is as directly available and as fully specific as information about anything else. J. J. Gibson has coined the term *visual proprioception* for the pick-up of self-specifying information from the optic array. Propriospecific information is not simply a matter of seeing one's own hands and body, important as this may be. (Under ordinary circumstances, the perceiver's hands are probably the most frequently available visual objects.) Even when no body parts are visible, optical flow patterns enable the perceiver to see where he is and where he is going. In short, the physical ego can be seen; it need not be inferred.

In the ordinary environment, information for visual proprioception is almost always available and almost always veridical. It can be simulated only by manipulating the entire optic array at once. A wide-screen film like Cinerama is one way to accomplish this; for laboratory purposes one can build an experimental room whose walls and ceiling move independently of the floor. Lee has used such a room to demonstrate the effectiveness of motion-produced optical flow.[13] A one-year-old child standing on the floor of the room will fall down if the walls are silently and suddenly moved forward a few inches, although nothing touches him. This is because the optical pattern produced by the moving walls would normally specify that the observer was plunging backward. The child compensates by shifting forward, overbalances, and falls. Even an adult who knows the experimental arrangement can be "knocked down" in this way if he is balancing on a narrow beam.

Information about oneself, like all other information, can only be picked up by an appropriately tuned schema. Conversely, all information that *is* picked up, including proprioceptive information, modifies a schema. In the case of movement through the environment, this is an orienting schema or cognitive map. This means that the cognitive map always includes the perceiver as well as the environment. Ego and world are perceptually inseparable.

Varieties of cognitive maps

It is not only mature, verbal, introspective organisms who have cognitive maps. Even very young children move around successfully in their homes, at least in the rooms where they often go and where important things are to be found. Huttenlocher's subject Craig is typical: at fifteen months when his only spoken words were "di" and "uhuh," he could be asked for a cookie while in the living room and would go to get it from the kitchen. Moreover, his orienting schema included readiness to perceive not only the permanent but also the temporary positions of things. "During this visit there is a pile of cookies on the living room floor which Craig has apparently spilled. We spend the latter part of the visit in the kitchen, where his mother says to him 'Do you want a cookie?'. He goes out of the kitchen and returns somewhat later, carrying the entire stack of cookies."[14] It is clear that Craig has accepted new information (the spilled cookies) into his cognitive map of the house, and that this enriched schema enabled him to find the cookies later. We have already seen that much younger infants can also retain information about the temporary location of objects, though for appreciably less time.

Craig's performance is not remarkable. It is typical not only of human infants but of many species of animals as well. The ability to find one's way in the environment and reach desired goals must be universally distributed; animals without this ability would hardly have survived the rigors of natural selection. As an example, consider Menzel's recent study of the chimpanzee's ability to remember the locations of hidden food.[15] The subjects of his experiments were a group of chimpanzees who had been living for more than a year in a natural outdoor enclosure. At the start of a test trial, the whole group was locked in a cage on the periphery of this field. One animal was taken out and carried around in the company of an experimenter who hid pieces of fruit in eighteen different places. During this phase, the chimpanzee could do nothing but watch and be carried. He was then returned to the group, and after two minutes all the animals were released. Menzel describes the typical result as follows:

> Usually, the test animal ran unerringly and in a direct line to the exact clump of grass or leaves, tree stump, or hole in the ground where a hidden food lay, grabbed the food, stopped briefly to eat, and then ran directly to the next place, no matter how distant or obscured by visual barriers that place was. . . . Each animal proceeded more or less in accordance with a "least distance" principle, and with no regard for the pathway along which the experimenters had carried him.[16]

Comparative psychology lies outside the scope of this book, so the achievements of Menzel's chimpanzees will not be considered further. They have been mentioned only to emphasize that cognitive maps are defined by information pickup and action, not by verbal description. Travel is one thing, travelogue another. A child can find his way around long before he can give an adequate account of where he has been or how he got there, just as he can do many other things that he is not fluent enough to describe. The later-appearing ability to describe orienting schemata is important in its own right, and we will consider it in Chapter 8. For the present, it may be useful to take it for granted, so that we can examine the structure of a complex example in some detail.

Sometimes an unfamiliar instance illustrates a point more vividly than a mundane one. Consider, therefore, the highly sophisticated orienting schemata developed by experts in a remote culture: the navigators of Puluwat Island in the Pacific Ocean. These men guide sailing canoes over hundreds of miles of open ocean, for trade or simply for pleasure. Their skill has long been admired by all who come into contact with them: by Western sailors and ethnologists as well by their neighbors in the Caroline Islands. Seeking a better understanding of what is evidently an extraordinary cognitive skill, the anthropologist Thomas Gladwin spent several months studying Puluwat navigation in 1967. He has described his findings in a beautiful book called *East is a Big Bird*,[17] on which the following account is based.

The Puluwatan navigator's skill has several components. Some of them concern the pickup of information from particularly subtle sources, which Gladwin calls *seamarks*. Slight changes in the color of the water indicate a deeply submerged reef, whose position is known; the rhythm of the water slapping the hull can be related to the several crisscrossing wave patterns characteristic of that part of the Pacific; the flight of birds suggests the probable direction of nearby islands. More interesting here, however, is the cognitive map into which this information is fed. It is based on a conceptual structure that the Puluwatans call *etak*. Though elegant and systematic, it is unlike any familiar Western way of representing motion through the environment.

Basic directions in etak are defined by the places around the horizon where particular stars rise. The navigator knows star courses between every pair of islands. (The eastward course from Puluwat to Truk, for example, is toward the rising position of the star Altair; Puluwatans call it "the big bird.") Unfortunately the stars themselves are not reliable sources of directional information; they cannot be seen by day or on cloudy nights, and even on clear nights they do not hover indefinitely over their rising positions. Moreover, it is often impossible to set a course straight toward one's destination. An unfavorable wind may require a series of tacks, fifty or a hundred miles long, in other directions. Thus the navigator must keep very close track of how far and in what direction he has come. He does not describe this progress in miles, however, nor with any measure of linear distance.

As the canoe proceeds in its voyage, it moves relative to nearby islands. (Nearby, in this context, generally means 50 or 100 miles away and far over the horizon.) One might also say, however, that the islands are moving relative to the canoe; the Puluwatans say exactly that. From the navigator's point of view, a particular *reference island* that he has in mind is constantly changing its star direction from the canoe. It may start out "under Altair," for example, and end under the Little Dipper (see Figure 5). In between, it "passes under" a series of other stars as the voyage progresses. Its successive star positions divide the voyage into corresponding segments or etaks. Position and distances are defined as if the canoe itself were stationary under the starry heaven while the reference island (there is one for each

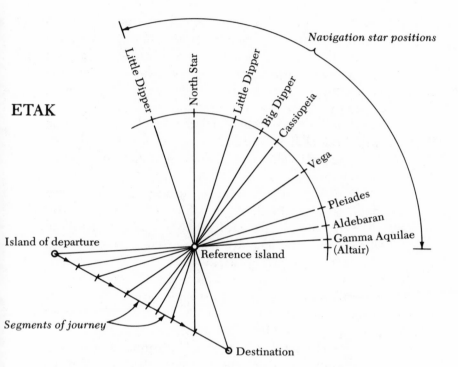

ETAK

Navigation star positions

Little Dipper
North Star
Little Dipper
Big Dipper
Cassiopeia
Vega
Pleiades
Aldebaran
Gamma Aquilae (Altair)

Island of departure
Reference island
Segments of journey
Destination

FIGURE 5. *Etak: the principle of navigation in Puluwat.* [From *East is a Big Bird* by T. Gladwin, 1970. Harvard University Press.]

inter-island passage) slid slowly backward. This method is used not only for the main course but for tacking; in that case it is the destination island that is said to move slowly past two or three star positions until the navigator has gone far enough and heads on the opposite tack.

Etak is the organizing principle of the cognitive map that makes the navigator's accomplishment possible. It functions, like all orienting schemata, to accept information and direct action; in this case, it guides visual search for expected seamarks and determines the heading on which the canoe must be sailed. Perceptual schemata are embedded in it because perceiving is a part of navigating. Leaving Puluwat by day the navigator sets his course by backsighting the island over the stern: certain trees, rocks, and so forth must be in line if he is on the proper course. He adjusts the canoe until these objects look right because then he knows he is sailing right. The same actions serve both perceiving and traveling.

The etak principle is highly abstract. The reference island is never in sight, and the star positions under which it "moves" are rarely visible either. Most of the relevant information really comes from dead reckoning, seamarks, wave patterns, and birds, but the navigator refers it to the imaginary movement of a remote island under the unmarked rising positions of invisible stars. It is not surprising that Westerners have had great difficulty in understanding such a system. They have sometimes concluded that the etak islands must be potential safety islands to which the navigator might sail in case of storm. Note the nature of this error: it is an overly concrete interpretation of the navigator's abstract idea. When remote islanders have made similar errors in interpreting *our* abstract notions, we have too often jumped to the conclusion that they were poorer thinkers than we are.

The image of the city

Cognitive maps are ubiquitous. We all know what to expect around the corner on the way home; we can all plan trips to a hundred destinations, and check our expectations along the way if we undertake one; we can all take new short cuts with some idea of where they lead. These abilities are commonplace, but they are by no means uninteresting. A particularly good account of them appears in Kevin Lynch's book *The Image of the City*.[18] Interviewing residents of Boston, Jersey City, and Los Angeles, Lynch asked what came to their minds first when they thought about the city, what they would encounter in traveling between two specific points, and many other questions. On the basis of the answers, and of rough sketch-maps his subjects drew, he discusses the "images" or cognitive maps that these cities engender.

Such cognitive maps typically include certain characteristic features. *Landmarks* such as towers, unusual building, or monuments, play an important role because they can be easily spotted from a distance. *Paths* are travelable routes—most often streets—by which the city dweller gets about, and *nodes* are salient points where several paths meet. *Districts* are regions of the city characterized by some easily recognized cultural or geographical property. Finally, *edges* are the visibly defined boundaries of districts or other areas: rivers, expressways, and the like. It is these features that define a city's structure as that structure is understood and used by its inhabitants.

Cognitive maps and perceptual schemata are related in two different ways that can both be illustrated by Lynch's analysis. First, a cognitive map *is* essentially a perceptual schema, though on a larger scale; it accepts information and guides exploration. Thus we should not be surprised to find that object schemata also include elements very similar to those Lynch describes. Hochberg has pointed out that this is often the case.[19]

Eye-movement recordings show that salient features of objects function as landmarks; they are visible from a long way off (i.e., in peripheral vision) and the eye often returns to them. The movements of our eyes are also significantly constrained by edges, especially by the real edges of objects. Moreover, it is obvious that most natural objects have subregions of particular significance that correspond to districts: the face of a person or the trunk of a tree. Only paths and nodes are missing, probably because of the *ballistic* nature of exploratory eye movements. Once the eye has been set in motion toward a new fixation point, it cannot change its path until it has arrived; little information will be picked up in midcourse. Thus the paths traversed by the eye do not offer the kind of continuous information that is essential for the development of a schema, and they go unnoticed in perception.

Landmarks and edges are real entities set in a real city; the corresponding perceptual schemata are similarly embedded in the cognitive map of that city. The schemata are not merely components of the map, however; they direct perception and pick up information in their own right. The city dweller knows how the critical features *look;* in other words, he knows how to look at them and roughly what he will see when he does. He also knows, in a general way, what he can expect to see as he approaches or traverses them. It is exactly for this reason that they are salient features for him. This illustrates a general feature of cognitive organization. Units at different "levels" are not just related sequentially, the lower ones feeding information to others further along; instead they are embedded, each engaging in its own cyclic relationship with environmentally available information.

One aspect of cognitive maps remains to be considered, and it may be the most intriguing of all. The city dweller does not use his orienting schema only in the course of traveling about; he can also use it when he is sitting quietly at home or being interviewed by a city planner. Such a schema can be detached from its original function and used as an independent source of information. One can imagine one's city as well as explore it. It is no accident that Lynch titled his book *The Image of the City*. There is a close relationship between cognitive maps and mental images, to which we must now turn.

Notes

1. I am following Gibson's (1966) terminology, in which perceptual systems are defined by the kind of information they pick up rather than by a particular end-organ. The auditory perceptual system, for example, includes the ears as mounted on the mobile head; the haptic system includes the skin, limbs, muscles, and joints as well as neural tissue.

2. A stationary head-restrained observer still has recourse to eye movements, and indeed he must make at least small ones if he is to continue seeing at all (artifically stabilized retinal images soon produce a total fade out of visual experience). Eye movements are no substitute for genuine exploration of the environment, however, because they do not provide new information about the relative positions of objects.

3. In a normally cluttered environment, even the smallest head movement brings some new portions of object-surfaces into view and conceals others. This results in the "accretion" or "deletion" (Kaplan, 1969) of elements of

microtexture belonging to some objects as they are dis-
occluded or occluded by others. Larger movements
occlude or disocclude entire objects or vistas.

4. J. J. Gibson (1966, p. 207).

5. Tolman (1948).

6. Downs and Stea (1973) have recently compiled a collection of readings on cognitive maps.

7. This point was made forcibly by Kevin Lynch, whose
   book *The Image of the City* (1960) was a landmark (!) or
   turning point (!) in the history of this field.

8. Boulding (1961, p. 3). This passage was also quoted by
   Miller, Galanter, and Pribram (1960).

9. This most common cognitive model is to be found in virtually every textbook: Lindsay and Norman (1972), Massaro (1975), Klatzky (1975), and also Neisser (1967). It has
   been particularly successful in accounting for the patterns
   of results obtained in tachistoscopic and reaction-time
   experiments (Sternberg, 1966, 1975; Posner and Mitchell,
   1967; Posner, Boies, Eichelman, and Taylor, 1969). Even
   in this domain, however, it has encountered serious difficulties in studies using categorizable or meaningful material (Jonides and Gleitman, 1972; Wheeler, 1970). Craik
   and Lockhart (1972) have tried to apply it to certain memory phenomena as well, arguing that words are remembered according to the "depth of processing" they have
   undergone. This approach too, has encountered difficulties (Craik and Tulving, 1975).

10. Recent elegant demonstrations of mutual support among
    current perceptual activities include the word-superiority
    effect (Wheeler, 1970; Johnston and McClelland, 1975); a
    similar effect with outline drawings and their compo-
    nents, reported by Weisstein and Harris (1974); and an
    effect of overall coherence on the tachistoscopic viewing
    of natural scenes (Biederman, 1972; Biederman, Glass,
    and Stacy, 1973).

11. A significant new technique for the hierarchical analysis
    of action sequences has recently been devised by
    Newtson (1976); it takes advantage of a spectator's ability
    to detect coherent units in the behavior of another person.

12. J. J. Gibson made this point in *Perception of the Visual World* (1950), and has amplified it in various ways since. Recent studies of optical flow patterns include Johnston, White, and Cumming (1973), Nakayama and Loomis (1974), Warren (in press).

13. Lee and Aronson (1974); Lishman and Lee (1973). An even simpler method is the "rotating shower curtain" illusion that has long been a staple of the psychological laboratory.

14. Huttenlocher (1974, p. 347).

15. Menzel (1973). Of course, there are a vast number of other cases. The long controversy about place-learning in rats, for example, eventually established to everyone's satisfaction that these animals use landmarks, take shortcuts, find their way to established goalsites from new starting positions, adopt revised modes of locomotion when old ones become impracticable, etc.

16. Menzel (1973, p. 943–944).

17. Gladwin (1970).

18. Lynch (1960). His book has given rise to a great deal of similar research on other cities and other aspects of cognitive maps. A summary of this work is available in Downs and Stea (1973). Lynch himself has extended his analysis to include the historical as well as the geographical aspects of urban life in *What Time is This Place?* (1972).

19. Hochberg (1975).

Imagining
and Remembering

A topic once regarded as too slippery, too mentalistic, and too unimportant for consideration, imagery has now become a fashionable area of cognitive research.[1] This has resulted in a number of important discoveries and rediscoveries. The effectiveness of images as aids to memory has been repeatedly confirmed; it has been established that imaging and perceiving can conflict with each other, at least under some conditions; the operations of scanning or rotating images have been shown to require regular and measurable amounts of time.[2] The eidetic imagery exhibited by certain unusual children has been intensively studied,[3] and books have been written about people who have remarkable imagery abilities.[4]

Much of this work has been interpreted in terms of the linear cognitive model caricatured in Figure 1. The model suggests that a visual image is essentially a "percept" that has been formed in an abnormal way. It is assumed that although percepts normally result from a processing sequence that begins with a stimulus, they can also be produced without any such trigger. A train of processes arising somehow in the middle of the perceptual apparatus instead of at the receptors can still be elaborated with the aid of memory and eventually reach the seat of consciousness. When this happens we supposedly experience a mental image. To use a bit of nineteenth-century terminology, images are nothing but "centrally excited sensations."

There are actually two versions of this theory, which differ about whether the flow of processing is finished when consciousness has been reached. Some psychologists suppose that the image can be manipulated, examined, or processed further after this point, as if it were a picture at which the subject were really looking.[5] This accords with our introspections in a certain sense, since we do seem to examine our images. On the other hand it has obvious philosophical disadvantages: a whole new perceptual apparatus must be hypothesized to do the looking. Impressed by this difficulty, other theorists prefer to suppose that all the processing is really done offstage, as it were, with the conscious image merely an epiphenomenal trace of work already accomplished.[6]

Both versions of the linear theory have some difficulty in explaining why images and percepts are not systematically confused with one another. How does the subject know whether the present content of his consciousness originated with an external stimulus? In fact, however, we almost always know this, at least when we are awake. Although an experiment by Perky is often cited as proving that percepts and images are confusable, it is seriously flawed and has not really been replicated.[7] Ordinary experience indicates that the opposite is true. Although perceiving an object and imaging it do have something in common, they are still easily distinguishable occurrences.

This chapter will suggest an approach to the problem that grows directly out of the account of perception given earlier. Imagining is not perceiving, but images are indeed derivatives of perceptual activity. In particular, they are the *anticipatory phases* of that activity, schemata that the perceiver has detached from the perceptual cycle for other purposes. Imagining is not normally confused with perceiving because the latter involves the continuing pickup of new information. It is only when that pickup is delayed or interrupted that imagery makes its appearance. Because this happens inevitably and regularly during locomotion, cognitive maps are the most widely used and least controversial kind of mental images.

Images as perceptual anticipations

In practice, the notion of *mental imagery* is defined by a loose assortment of operations that include one's own introspection, other people's reports of their introspection, and a variety of more or less objective experimental procedures. The present hypothesis is intended to apply not only to the experimental results, but also to many of the introspectively-given phenomena. I believe that the experience of having an image is just the inner aspect of a readiness to perceive the imagined object, and that differences in the nature and quality of people's images reflect differences in the kind of information they are prepared to pick up. Some people find it natural to say they "see" their images, while others reject this terminology altogether. It is hard to know how much these individual differences are due to accidental choices of metaphor and how much they reflect real differences among people's visual systems. If images are instances of perceptual readiness, however, one would certainly expect to find differences in the accuracy, scope, and detail of the information they anticipate.

Imagining and seeing are fundamentally different. The cognitive maps and object schemata that appear as images when they stand alone tend to blend into the acts of locomotion and perception when they occur during ongoing activity. They are only parts of the perceptual cycle, not the whole cycle and not its object. The experience we have when they do stand alone is imagining, not seeing. Everyone has such experiences, whatever he may call them and whatever level of structure or detail they may represent. Images are not reproductions or copies of earlier percepts, because perceiving is not a matter of having percepts in the first place. Images are not pictures in the head, but plans for obtaining information from potential environments.

On this view, human beings are not the only creatures endowed with mental imagery. Every organism that can anticipate the arrangement of things in its environment has cognitive maps; everyone who can make ready to pick up information specifying a certain object can imagine that object. This must include a great many kinds of animals as well as very young children. It also includes articulate adults, however, and their introspective reports pose a pair of problems for the hypothesis. The first problem is created by the very existence of introspection: if images are anticipations rather than pictures, what is going on when we describe them? This question must be postponed to the next chapter, which is explicitly concerned with language and description. The other problem is more pressing, and may have troubled the reader already. It is obvious from everyone's introspection that we can imagine things which, in fact, we do not expect. The very word *imaginary* suggests that images are anything but realistic anticipations of the future. How can this be understood?

When someone describes a mental image, on this hypothesis, the thing he is talking about does not exist in some separate and shadowy realm of the mind; it is actually or potentially a perceivable thing in the world. This does not mean, however, that it must be real. By their nature, anticipations concern things that only might come to pass rather than things whose existence is already established. Moreover, there is no reason why someone who has an image must believe that the corresponding object is just around the corner or could ever actually appear before him. To imagine something that you know to be unreal, it is only necessary to detach your visual readinesses from your general notions of what will really happen and embed them in schemata of a different sort. When you have an image of a unicorn at your elbow—while quite certain that unicorns are purely mythical animals—you are making ready to pick up the visual information that the unicorn would provide, despite being fully aware that your preparations are in vain. I do not know whether animals are capable of these schematic rearrangements; certainly children take a good deal of time to master them. In any case, they seem to be easy enough for adults. According to the hypothesis being proposed, however, even counterfactual images are still potentially functional anticipations. If the right kind of unicorn were somehow to materialize at the elbow of a person who was imagining one, he would see it more quickly and easily than if he had been imagining anything else. Experimental evidence that supports this prediction will be considered below.

In a sense, imagining a unicorn involves two simultaneous and contradictory anticipations: of seeing it and of not seeing it. While the first of these is being developed by visual schemata, the second is maintained by deeper and less labile cognitive systems. They need not be at odds; the visual schemata are usually embedded in the others and partially controlled by them. We can imagine things deliberately, for reasons that have little or nothing to do with our perceptible environment. Sometimes the reasons are obvious enough; an experimenter may even have asked us to conjure up an image because his study requires that we do so. Often, however, we can give little or no account of the reason why something has come to mind. Mental images frequently symbolize anticipations or wishes that are preconscious or unconscious, in Freud's sense of those terms. These symbolic processes will not be considered further here, however; my present concern is with the nature of imagery rather than its purpose.[8]

The ability to divide, detach, and manipulate our own anticipations is immensely important. It is, I believe, the fundamental operation in all so-called higher mental processes. Imagery is only one example; in the next chapter I will argue that language is another. How does this detachment come about? There are many ways,

ᴏꜰ which are offered to us—and demanded of
ᴜs—by the practices and institutions of the culture in
which we grow up. The higher mental processes are
primarily social phenomena, made possible by cognitive tools and characteristic situations that have evolved
in the course of history. Mental imagery, however,
represents at least a partial exception to this rule. Detachment of images from the immediate context occurs
inevitably in at least one situation with which we are
all familiar: locomotion.

Chapter 6 emphasized that cognitive maps are essentially orienting schemata, similar in function to the less
extensive schemata that enable us to perceive objects.
Nevertheless, there is an important difference between
them. The successive phases of the perceptual cycle
succeed one another rapidly, often in fractions of a second. Perceiving takes time but not much; the anticipations, adjustments, and glances which occupy that time
are brief indeed. Locomotion, on the other hand, is a
slow business. There are inevitably prolonged periods
during which the moving person is anticipating objects
and places that have not yet come into view. This means
he is often in the position of sustaining schemata quite
inappropriate to his immediate environment or to anything he is about to do. Under these conditions an
increasingly detached use of orienting schemata must
become commonplace. As a result, there is considerable consensus about what cognitive maps are like; far
more than about images in the narrower sense. Another
by-product of this situation is that everyone can use
orienting schemata for purposes other than locomotion,
at least after the possibility of doing so has been pointed
out. This possibility underlies the world's oldest and
most powerful mnemonic device.

The Method of Loci

Any animal that can find its way around in the world is ipso facto exhibiting an effective and versatile kind of memory. At every moment in its travels it anticipates information not then available, on the basis of a cognitive map developed on some earlier occasion. That orienting schemata is further altered at every moment in ways that will leave their mark the next time it is used. These abilities are fundamental to adaptive behavior in human beings as well as in rats and chimpanzees, but we know surprisingly little about them. How are cognitive maps acquired? What sorts of information do they incorporate at various stages in their development? How are they altered by experience? Under what conditions are they forgotten? What kinds of similarity lead to confusion between orienting schemata for different environments? In the absence of experimental answers to most of these questions,[9] only a few vague generalizations can be offered here.

It is evidently easy to add new information to our cognitive maps when we perceive some change in the environment: that the bridge is closed for repairs, or that the cat has fallen asleep on the sofa. Such information is remarkably durable and easily recalled, although the degree of detail involved varies greatly from one occasion to the next and from one person to the next. (Some of the variation simply reflects differences in how much information was picked up in the first place.) It is particularly important that we can add information to cognitive maps even when we are merely told about situational changes without perceiving them ourselves. We can alter our perceptual anticipations and our travel plans on the basis of verbal information alone.

Changes produced in this way are not equivalent to those that direct perception would bring about, because we have not engaged in a perceptual cycle with the objects themselves. Nevertheless, they can be substantial and permanent.

To some extent, cognitive maps may be subject to forgetting; that is, they may lose detail with time. Forgetting in this sense is less powerful than one might suppose, however; we may discover with pleasure that we can still find our way around once-familiar terrain even after many years. The forgetting that does occur tends to affect minor details of embedded schemata rather than the overall embedding structure. At least this is what would be predicted on the basis of analogous work with verbal material, where the overall meaning of a sentence or a story survives far longer than the particular words that established it.[10]

Most of the errors that occur in the use of cognitive maps are probably due not so much to general "forgetting" as to a kind of confusion or interference. Often we have formed more than one cognitive map of a particular part of the environment. The last time we saw them, for example, the bridge may have been open to traffic and the cat on the rug. Under those conditions, proper recall would require knowing which cognitive map is presently appropriate; that is, which one was formed more recently. If no surviving characteristic of the cognitive maps indicates their relative recency (as must often be the case after a lapse of time), mistakes will occur. Route finding and recall are therefore most susceptible to error in situations that have frequently changed (like the locations of cats) and least in situations that are relatively stable (like the locations of buildings).

The fact that cognitive maps are relatively long last-
ing and yet easily modifiable makes them useful for
mnemonic purposes. The Method of Loci, invented by
the Greeks in ancient times, takes advantage of those
characteristics. The user begins by familiarizing himself with a series of particular locations along some
route or path. (For the Ancients this was often a walk
through a large temple that had many distinctive niches
and statues; nowadays a university campus is more con-
venient.) Once learned, such a cognitive map can be
used over and over again for mnemonic purposes. To
commit an arbitrary list of things to memory, you simply
visualize the successive items as if they were situated at
the consecutive loci already established. To recall
them, you need only take a mental stroll along the path;
they will all be found resting comfortably in their
places.[11]

There is no doubt about the effectiveness of this
method. It allows the user to memorize a list of any
length in a single trial, provided he has previously established a cognitive map with enough distinct loci. It
works for everyone, even for people who begin by de-
nying that they have mental images at all. After many
class demonstrations, I have yet to find a student unable
to use it. Some years ago a group of my students devised
and taught a course on memory and imagination in a
local junior high school; the Method of Loci was understood and employed by every pupil.[12]

The universal effectiveness of this mnemonic system
is easily explained. Our image of an object in a particular place is simply a readiness to pick up information
specifying the object when we get to the place. Anyone
familiar with a particular environment has a cognitive
map in which the schemata of many individual loci are

embedded and can anticipate what he would see at each of these places in turn. Anyone who can change a cognitive map on the basis of verbal information, and later give verbal descriptions of what he is ready to see, can use the Method of Loci to organize and recall arbitrary lists.

Association, imagery, and memory

There are other ways to use images for remembering things. In the experimental procedure called "paired associates," the subject studies a large number of word pairs (for example *shark-crib*) until he can recall the second member of any pair as soon as the first member is shown. A list of twenty such pairs must be repeated many times if it is to be learned by conventional means. Learning is very much faster if the subject is told to form mental images of each pair of objects in interaction: to visualize a shark *in* a crib or *eating* a crib. The method will not work if the two objects are simply imagined loosely side by side; they must be in some sort of relationship. Moreover, it is of little use if the pairs to be learned consist of abstract words like *justice* or *category*; they must be concrete.[13]

These mnemonic devices are based on object schemata, just as the Method of Loci is based on orienting schemata. Perceiving, like locomotion, is a cyclic activity that includes anticipation and information pickup. Any delay between the anticipation and the pickup creates a state of unfulfilled perceptual readiness, and the inner aspect of that active schema is a mental image. To conjure up an image of a shark in a crib is simply to prepare oneself to look at one, making ready to pick up

the information that such an unlikely spectacle
would offer.

It is important to note that a real shark in a real crib
would offer different information from a shark seen
alone: the bars would occlude parts of his body, even
though a slight movement of the perceiver's head might
suffice to bring them into view again. When two objects
are in a close spatial relationship, the perceptual cycle
takes a different course than it would if each were seen
by itself. Consequently our schema of a given object
becomes modified when we anticipate seeing it in some
particular context. All of us make such modifications
every day. The fact that I left my favorite pipe in the
ashtray in the living room, for example, means that my
most recent plans for looking at it also included looking
at (or around, or through) that ashtray. When I now try to
recall where I left it, my schema of the pipe reflects
those perceptual plans; i.e., it is an image of the pipe in
the ashtray. If I owned only one pipe and had left it
behind only once, I could not possibly fail to recall
where it was on this basis.

I often do fail, of course. The method can succeed
only if the proper schema is evoked at the time of recall:
my pipe in that particular ashtray, the shark in the crib
and not the shark in the ad for "Jaws." Where many
schemata exist, what distinguishes the right one? Often
additional context (embedding schemata) serves this
purpose, as when I remember smoking the pipe while
talking with my wife earlier in the evening. Also it is
usually easy to distinguish a recently formed schema,
perhaps because some of its internal context—
underlying attitudes, plans, feelings—continue into the
time when one tries to remember. If these kinds of information are missing, one will probably forget. That

may be why professional mnemonists advise the use of bizarre, unusual images rather than mundane ones. Although some recent experiments have failed to find any advantage of bizarreness in mnemonic devices,[14] I am skeptical of their results. Such experiments typically use naive subjects for whom the whole situation necessarily creates a unique context, and they have usually tested for immediate rather than delayed recall.

This interpretation of image mnemonics explains why the objects in question must be imagined as interacting rather than as simply existing side by side. Two objects interact, in the sense used here, if their spatial relationship makes a difference for how they look, or for how we would look at them. It is better to visualize the shark inside the crib rather than simply next to it because only the former relationship changes our schema for perceiving sharks. The hypothesis also explains why the words to be associated must be concrete rather than abstract. More precisely, it offers a definition of *concrete* which is applicable to this task. A word is concrete if and only if it denotes something that one can perceive, i.e., something that provides sensory information of a kind that can be anticipated. (Of course, we can use image mnemonics for abstract words if we somehow relate them to concrete ones, perhaps remembering "justice–category" by visualizing a gory cat on a pair of scales.)

By its very nature, a schema can represent things that are temporarily concealed. Although your overcoat may be in your closet, for example, you can anticipate some of the information that would become available if you went to the closet and opened the door. In this way, one can imagine objects that are concealed inside or behind other objects as well as things in plainly visible interaction. If images were mental pictures, this would not be true: no ordinary picture can reveal an interior object. If they are anticipations, however, they need not be limited to what can be seen from a single station point. It follows that memory should be aided just as much if one imagines a concealing, unpicturable relation between two things as a picturable one. Nancy Kerr and I were able to show some years ago that this is the case.[15] Although our subjects reported introspectively that their images of concealed objects were less "vivid" or "good" than other images, the former were no less effective mediators for memory than the latter.

The deliberate use of mental images is only one way of remembering things, but the principles by which I have tried to explain it are quite general. It is tempting to think that a full-fledged theory of memory might be constructed along the same lines. In such a theory, repeated presentation of the same material would constitute a regularity to be detected, rather than a way of strengthening an individual memory trace. Since schemata do not disappear, their use (detached or not) could account for remembering; forgetting would occur whenever the present input was not specific enough to specify a schema unequivocally. With a few supplementary hypotheses (special properties of verbal schemata would be needed to explain laboratory short-term memory, for example), this conception could probably deal with many familiar experimental phenomena: context effects, encoding specificity, proactive inhibition and its release, category clustering, and the like. Nevertheless, the temptation will be resisted. No theory of memory will be offered in this book.

The fact is that we have almost no systematic knowledge about memory as it occurs in the course of ordinary life. Almost all the phenomena that a contemporary theory must explain are highly artificial: recall of word

lists or nonsense syllables, identification of photo-
graphs that were included in a long series inflicted
on the subject earlier, and so on. Bartlett recognized
this problem many years ago,[16] but his demands for
specific recall of page-long "stories" read on previous
occasions were almost equally unrealistic. Contemporary neo-Bartlettians are again setting their subjects the
task of remembering brief texts,[17] but the ingenuity of
their methods does not alter the fact that no ordinary
person would do such a thing if he could help it.
(People do read books, of course, but psychologists
have rarely studied what they know as a result of doing
so.[18] Actors memorize lines, but not by the methods
used in these experiments.) There is new interest in
how children develop mnemonic skills,[19] but it is
chiefly focused on artificial tasks that require highly
specific strategies. Cross-cultural research has made it
clear that these strategies are somehow a by-product of
formal education,[20] but we still do not know how or
why. More important, we still have almost no systematic information about how a person remembers events
he has witnessed (though some modern research on this
question has begun to appear[21]), people he has met,
messages he must carry, or where he has left his pipe.
Until we know more about memory in the natural contexts where it develops and is normally used, theorizing
is premature.

Touch and taste

So far, the discussion of images and memory has centered on visual images and anticipations of looking.
This is not inappropriate, since visual images have been
the most commonly studied and probably the most

widely used mnemonic devices. Nevertheless, a few remarks about other sensory systems may not be out of place.

Much of the information about our environment that we usually get by looking could also be obtained by haptic exploration. We can discover many of the properties of nearby objects, as well as their layout, by touching and feeling them. Since these kinds of information can be anticipated, they can be incorporated in cognitive maps and images. I do not mean that haptic information is somehow recoded into a visual form, but that schemata direct explorations in several modalities concurrently, developing relevant anticipations for all of them. To be sure, as sighted persons it is primarily with our eyes that we determine where something is located, because vision provides the most accessible and the most accurate information about spatial relations. It is with our hands, however, that we discover an object's makeup, texture, and weight, and its response to touch or pressure. All of these properties can be represented by images without regard to their sensory origin. Our perceptual anticipations are so thoroughly integrated that things may come to look hard or rough or heavy (although the definitive information about these properties comes through touch) and to feel an inch wide (although experiments have shown that in case of conflict, the decisive information about size and position is usually visual.[22]) The perception of objects and events is the fundamental process, and it uses whatever information is available.

These considerations suggest that although cognitive maps are a species of images, they need not be visual. Blind persons can also have orienting schemata; indeed they must have them if they are to get about. They surely also have images of individual objects, i.e., anticipations of information that they might obtain by exploring the objects haptically. It follows that they should be able to use mental images as aids to associative memory, just as sighted people do. Recent research with congenitally blind subjects indicates that this is true.[23]

Before leaving this topic, I will speculate briefly about the mnemonic role of still another sensory system, that of taste. It seems possible that taste is a somewhat more passive sense than vision or touch. Once a substance is in the mouth, the information obtained by tasting it is probably much the same no matter what the taster may do. Even though one can develop refined anticipations of taste (a good chef knows how his ingredients will taste in a new combination), the gustatory experience itself is not very manipulable. This may help to explain the peculiarly vivid familiarity of a flavor tasted once again after a long interval, and its alleged capacity to bring back a flood of memories.[24] Because vision depends on schema-directed explorations, we rarely see the same object in exactly the same way twice. If the second visual encounter occurs long after the first, the relevant schemata will almost certainly have changed in the meantime; we will look at the object differently and pick up at least slightly different information. If tastes are obtained more passively, however, two widely separated tastings of the same substance might be nearly identical, and might thus lead to a particularly vivid experience of recognition.

Manipulating the image

If images are anticipations, they should facilitate subsequent perception. Perceptual readiness is not a minor by-product of visualizing, but its essence. To have a perceptual set for something is to have an image. The more precisely that image anticipates the information to come, the more effective the set should be. This has often been shown; a particularly striking demonstration was recently devised by Michael Posner and his colleagues.[25] A subject who has just seen a given letter, say A, will identify another A as the same letter more quickly if it appears in exactly the same form as before, but more slowly if it now appears in lower case. A similar facilitation occurs even when the subject is not shown but merely *told* what the coming letter will be, so that he can imagine it in advance.

Posner explains these and similar results by postulating a cognitive structure he calls a "visual code" of the letter.[26] Letters are identified by being matched to such codes, and an appropriate preexposure can place a particular code in readiness. It is obvious that the notions of *code* and *schema* have much in common, and it may be difficult to distinguish between them in experiments of this kind. The advantage of *schema* is that it generalizes easily to natural, continuous viewing, in which the perceiver himself actively seeks information over a period of time. Indeed, it was to account for this kind of active perception that the concept was introduced. A code, in contrast, seems to be a passive detection device; it and its owner can only wait patiently for the proper stimulus configuration to appear. I suspect that the particular properties of codes that have been inferred from reaction time experiments—their latencies, their organization in serial or parallel structures—will turn out to have little generality.

If images are anticipatory schemata, they should be accompanied by anticipatory behavior. In particular, it would not be surprising to find that people move their eyes in ways appropriate for picking up information about imagined objects or events. This proposition is not easy to test with ordinary images, because the eye movements we make in looking at most things are not determinate. Someone who looks at a chair may fixate the seat, scan the back, look at each leg in turn, or carry out many other kinds of visual exploration. Even when a natural pattern of scanning exists, the skilled imaginer need not follow it. Though in one sense he is ready to see the object, he knows perfectly well that it will not appear. Which anticipation actually controls his eye movements will depend on many factors: his overall plans and intentions, his experience with counterfactual imaging, the dominance of one particular scanning pattern for the events in question, etc. Experimentally, it has been shown that people who imagine systematic *motions*, like those of a table tennis match, do tend to make eye movements in the expected pattern.[27] The same principle applies to dreamers, as one might expect. Although there are obviously other determinants of the rapid eye movements of dreamers as well (they have been observed in neonates, decorticated cats, and congenitally blind subjects), these movements have sometimes been found to correspond to the imaginary content of the dream.[28] Of course, the dreamer does not first see an imaginary object and then move his eyes to examine it. He anticipates seeing something, plans to look at it, and then executes as much of his plan as he can.

These considerations explain why images sometimes interfere with perception, and vice versa. Visualizing one thing and looking at another is just as difficult as looking at two things simultaneously—which, as we noted in Chapter 5, may be difficult indeed. Interference of this sort was first demonstrated by Brooks,[29] who showed that subjects cannot easily make a visually guided response while describing a visual form from memory, nor manipulate a mental image while reading directions. His findings have been repeatedly confirmed.[30] There have also been some (disputed) demonstrations that directed visual activity interferes with the use of visual images as mnemonics.[31] Such results are generally taken to mean that imagery uses some of the same "mechanisms" as perception. The present hypothesis makes this interpretation more specific. Perception is a cyclic activity that includes an anticipatory phase; imagery is anticipation occurring alone.

The anticipation hypothesis explains another interesting experimental result. Kosslyn[32] has measured how quickly people can report on minor details of an imagined object; he found faster responses for objects imagined as large or close than for those imagined small or far away. He interprets his findings to mean that a large mental image is essentially like a big (and hence easily examined) picture, while a small image is like a little picture that must be enlarged before it can be used. This is by no means the only possible interpretation. It seems to me that plans for looking at distant or small objects are necessarily different from those for examining things that are large and near at hand. Searching for small details is compatible with the latter plans, but not the former. Subjects who are asked to imagine small details while they are visualizing a faraway or minified object are essentially in an interference situation, like those devised by Brooks.

Before concluding this chapter, we must consider one last set of imagery experiments, perhaps the most ingenious of all. These are the studies of imagined rotations conducted by Shepard, Cooper, and their collaborators.

In the first of these studies, subjects were shown two pictures of geometrical objects and asked whether the same object was depicted in both. The two objects were often oriented differently so that the subject had to rotate one of them mentally before he could determine whether it was identical to the other. The resulting reaction times were a linear function of the degree of rotation: the greater the difference between the orientations of the two objects, the slower was the response.[33] The subjects were apparently carrying out mental rotations at a fixed rate of speed.

Subsequent studies have tapped this process of mental rotation in a different way. In these studies the stimulus is a capital letter (or a specific but meaningless shape) whose identity is known in advance. On any given trial, the subject need only report whether it is being shown in normal or mirror-image form; this determination is made difficult because it may be presented at any orientation from 0° to 360°. At the beginning of each trial the subject develops an image of the normal form and begins to rotate it in his mind at a regular rate; the real form is then shown at an unpredicted instant. It turns out that his decision time depends on how much the real orientation of the suddenly presented form deviates from the orientation attained by his visual image in the same instant.[34]

To understand these results, consider how actual rotating objects are perceived. Suppose, for example, that we want to look at an acrobat's face as he spins in a somersault. This requires a schema that accepts information about the speed and direction with which the acrobat is turning, and directs the pickup of information from the position where his head will be at the next moment. Any perceiver who can do this successfully will also be able to imagine such a spin simply by activating the anticipatory schema in the absence of the acrobat. His image then consists of a readiness to pick up certain kinds of information from a given part of a moving body. This readiness is precisely what the experiments demonstrate: subjects pick up information most quickly at the orientation they already have in mind. As Cooper has put it, ". . . during a mental rotation, the internal process passes through a series of states at each one of which the subject is especially prepared for the presentation of a particular external object in a particular orientation."[35]

I am less sure why the rotation of the expectancy should take place at such a slow and regular rate in these studies. We can generally shift our images around us as we please without regard for real distances: it takes me no longer to visualize a house once seen in England than one in New York. The reason for the constant rate must lie somehow in the requirement that an image be maintained even while it is being changed: *this* letter or *this* object must be rotated to a new position. Perhaps future research will clarify the problem.

Notes

1. A number of recent books attest to this interest: Richardson (1969), Horowitz (1970), Segal (1971[b]), Paivio (1971), Sheehan (1972), Chase (1973).
2. Specific references for these experimental findings will appear later in this chapter.

3. Eidetic imagery in children—the child's report that he
   continues to see a picture for a minute or so after it has
   been removed from the field of view—remains controversial. Haber and Haber, who reinvigorated the study of
   eidetic imagery with their 1964 paper, have revised some
   of their views on the basis of new evidence (Leask, Haber
   and Haber, 1969). Different studies have reported widely
   varying results on such basic issues as the incidence of
   eidetic imagery, its accuracy, and the extent to which it is
   really similar to the experience of seeing. Gray and
   Gummerman (1975) offer a useful summary of this work.
   For my part, I think it most likely that eidetic children
   have mental images much like those of other people but
   are interested in different aspects of them and have come
   to use a different mode of introspective description and
   metaphor. The phenomenon has apparently never been
   found in adults except in cross-cultural testing situations,
   where problems of translation, criterion, social expectations, and mixed metaphors are probably responsible for
   the remarkable variety and inconsistency of the results
   (Doob, 1964, 1965, 1966, 1970; Feldman, 1968). Amazing
   visual memories have occasionally been observed in
   adult subjects where these problems of communication
   are not at issue (e.g., Luria, 1968; Stromeyer, 1970;
   Stromeyer and Psotka, 1970; Gummerman and Gray,
   1971), but they seem to be very different from childhood
   eidetic imagery as well as from one another. The images
   of such subjects do not simply outlast the stimulus for a
   few seconds and then fade, but can be recalled at will. I
   can offer no useful theoretical account of them.
4. Luria (1968).
5. For example, Kosslyn (1975). Most theorists shy away
   from stating the picture theory outright, but it is
   often implicit.
6. For example, Pylyshyn (1973). Bower, who once held
   something like the examinable-picture view (Bower,
   1972) has now apparently discarded it and agrees that the
   real cognitive mechanisms are elsewhere (Anderson and
   Bower, 1973).
7. Perky (1910) asked naive subjects to "project" some par-

ticular mental image onto a screen where a genuine optical image of the same object was being surreptitiously displayed. Many did describe this real picture as being their own image, but the demand characteristics of the situation left them little choice. (Subjects who suspected the trick were discarded.) Segal (1971[a], 1972), who tried repeatedly to replicate Perky's results, found occasional cases of stimulus "incorporation" into the image, but few if any where subjects mistook a real picture for an imagined one.

8. The symbolic functions of imagery are discussed briefly in Chapter 6 of *Cognitive Psychology* (1967).

9. Research on cognitive maps has recently been reviewed by Siegel and White (1975); several important studies have been contributed by H. L. Pick and his collaborators (Kosslyn, Pick, and Fariello, 1974; Acredolo, Pick, and Olsen, 1975). Some of the research inspired by Kevin Lynch's work (Chapter 6, note 18) is also relevant. Studies of memory for "micro-environments"—toy layouts or pictures of them—may have something to offer (Mandler and Stein, 1974; Mandler and Parker 1976; Dirks and Neisser, in press), and there is also an older literature on "finger mazes."

10. Sachs (1967, 1974) showed that subjects forget the details of individual sentences almost immediately while preserving their semantic import; Bransford and his collaborators that one recognizes the scenario established by a string of sentences rather than the sentences themselves (Bransford and Franks, 1971; Bransford, Barclay, and Franks, 1972); Tulving and Thomson (1973) that even the recognition of isolated words may depend on reestablishing the particular mental context present at the time of learning.

11. Yates (1966) provides a fascinating history of the method of loci from classical times to the present. Ross and Lawrence (1968) offered the first modern experimental proof of its effectiveness. Bower's "Analysis of a mnemonic device" (1970) gives a highly readable account of recent research on the method and related mnemonic devices, together with some speculation on their neurophysiologi-

cal basis. Every "how-to" book on memory includes either the method of loci itself or some modification of it (e.g., Furst, 1948; Lorayne & Lucas, 1974).

12. A brief account of this course appears in Neisser (1975).

13. Overall reviews of the work appear in Paivio (1971) and Bower (1972). Especially convincing demonstrations of the effectiveness of imagery in learning paired associates are those of Bobrow and Bower (1969) and Aiken (1971). For an interesting application to school learning, see Atkinson (1975).

14. Collyer, Jonides, and Bevan (1972); Wollen, Weber, and Lowry (1972); Nappe and Wollen (1973).

15. Neisser and Kerr (1973).

16. Bartlett (1932).

17. Important modern studies of memory for prose include those of Sachs (1967, 1974), Dooling and Lachman (1971), Bransford and Franks (1971), Bransford and Johnson (1973), Paris and Carter (1973). All follow Bartlett's emphasis on meaning and understanding as crucial for memory. Jenkins (1974) has presented a forceful statement of a "contextualist" theory which attempts to integrate this work. More recently, Rumelhart has elaborated a rather precise schema theory of how brief stories are understood and remembered (Rumelhart, in press; Rumelhart and Ortony, in press).

18. A recent study at Cornell (Neisser and Hupcey, 1975) represents a stab in this direction.

19. See, for example, Flavell (1970); Brown (1975); Kreutzer, Leonard, and Flavell (1975).

20. Cole, Gay, Glick, and Sharp (1971); Scribner and Cole (1973); Scribner (1974).

21. Loftus and Palmer (1974); Loftus (1975).

22. This is the upshot of most experiments on visual "disarrangement" (e.g. Harris, 1967; Rock & Harris, 1965).

23. Jonides, Kahn, and Rozin (1975).

24. Although Proust celebrated this characteristic of taste long ago, there are no experiments to confirm it. I have, however, met people who report such experiences.

25. The basic conditions governing this type of perceptual set were explored by Posner, Boies, Eichelman, and Taylor (1969); an important variation was offered by Beller (1971). For a survey of work with this and related methods see Posner (1973[b]). Of course, the capital/small letter paradigm was not the first demonstration of perceptual set by any means; it has been a staple of the psychological laboratory for years. For reviews of work in this tradition, see Haber (1966) or my 1967 book.

26. Posner (1973[a]).

27. Antrobus, Antrobus, and Singer (1964).

28. Koulack (1972) has recently reviewed the experimental evidence for a correspondence between eye movements and dream content.

29. Brooks (1967, 1968).

30. Segal and Fusella (1970), Byrne (1974), Salthouse (1974, 1975).

31. The original demonstration of this by Atwood (1971) has not always been easy to replicate. However, Janssen (in press) has recently obtained a similar result several times under what seem to be well-controlled conditions.

32. Kosslyn (1975).

33. Shepard and Metzler (1971); Metzler and Shepard (1974). Just and Carpenter (in press) have recently shown that subjects look back and forth between the two figures more often when there are larger angular discrepancies. This is just the sort of exploratory activity that would be expected on the present view. Nevertheless, I doubt that the eye movements are essential aspects of mental rotation; like eye motions in other kinds of images, they are products of schematic activity rather than its cause.

34. Cooper and Shepard (1973); Cooper (1975, 1976; Cooper and Podgorny, in press). Hochberg and Gellman (1976) have shown that such mental rotation rates depend on the availability of landmarks (in Lynch's sense) in the displays, though they do not necessarily vary with the complexity of the form.

35. Cooper (1976, p. 296).

Perceiving
and Using Speech

I approach the topic of language with considerable hesitation. Linguistics is an intimidating science, and even its uncertain stepchild "psycholinguistics" has already produced a formidable body of research and theory. Although I would not venture to survey either of these disciplines, their subject matter cannot be entirely ignored. Two aspects of linguistic skill will be treated here. First, since speech is something perceivable, we will consider what kinds of information it offers to the prepared listener. Second, since speech can refer not only to real present events but also to images and other introspectively given ones, we will consider how its referential function might originate and how it might be extended to perceptual anticipations.

Sounds inform us about events. While vision and touch enable us to explore stationary environments, hearing tells us only about movement and change. With a few exceptions like thunder, natural sounds are always produced by objects in motion (echoes are a special case). Things vibrate, or bang into each other, or rub across one another; we hear footsteps and wingbeats, rumbles and scratches, splashes and clangs. The sounds *specify* these events. The acoustic pattern that reaches our ears is specific to the identity, location, motion and meaning of the sounding objects, just as the optic array is specific to the objects that reflected the light. This acoustic information can be picked up by a perceiver if he knows how to listen for it, i.e., if he has properly attuned and continuously accommodating schemata that can accept the information as it becomes available and ready themselves for what may come next.

If this is true of natural sound in general, it must also be true of the sounds of speech. They represent information, but about what?

There are really two answers to this question, because speech is informative about two different classes of events. First, there are the things the speaker is talking about. Speech certainly conveys information about these things; that is its primary function. Second, however, (and ontogenetically first) there are the physical events that give rise to the speech sounds themselves. They are not at all mysterious; an entire branch of science—articulatory phonetics—is devoted to their study. The sounds of speech are produced in people's mouths by movements of certain parts of the body known as the *articulators,* especially the tongue, cheeks, and lips.

To be sure, this is an oversimplification. The sound really originates lower in the vocal tract, with the exhalation of air and its passage across the vibrating vocal cords. By the time it reaches the world outside the mouth, however, it has been "shaped" by the changing configuration of the articulators, which themselves were more literally shaped by the muscular activity of the speaker. To speak is to make finely controlled movements in certain parts of your body, with the result that information about these movements is broadcast to the environment. For this reason the movements of speech are sometimes called *articulatory gestures.*

A person who perceives speech, then, is picking up information about a certain class of real, physical, tangible (as we shall see) events that are occurring in someone's mouth. These are not random events, of course: they have meaning. The speaker moves his articulators in the course of uttering words—or, at another level, ideas—and it is only in this wider context that their movements become predictable or coherent. It is just this level of coherence that explains why the listener seems to hear words and meanings rather than the articulatory events themselves; they are the coinage of his anticipations. We have already considered a similar situation in vision. The perception of a visually specified event, such as a smile, depends on the particular cycle in which the perceiver is engaged. It is one thing to develop readinesses based on the meaning of the smile (perhaps looking for other signs of a friendly disposition) and quite another to seek more information about the temporary geometry of the smiler's face. As it turns out, the former is much easier to do than the latter.

The same principle applies to speech. It is far more natural to develop anticipations about articulatory events in terms of their syntax and meaning than of their kinematics; so much more natural, in fact, that it seems almost vulgar to mention the latter at all.

Nevertheless, the fact that speech is a real physical event has important consequences for the way we experience it. The basic successive units of which speech is composed, the *phonemes,* are better defined by the motions of the articulators than by any simple acoustical properties. The standard example used to illustrate this state of affairs is that of the stop consonants: /d/, /t/, /b/, etc. Though these consonants are easily identified by listeners regardless of the vowel that happens to follow them, they are far from easy to define in acoustical terms. "Dig" and "Do," for example, are unambiguously heard as beginning with the same phoneme, /d/. If we examine the acoustic waveforms or the spectrograms of these words, however, it is far from clear what is the same about them; they begin quite differently. Nor can we capture the essence of /d/ by tape recording the words and cutting off pieces from the end until only /d/ remains; once the vowels are gone, nothing is left on the tape but a variety of odd-sounding chirps.[1] It is much easier to understand what a /d/ might be if we consider the articulatory gesture that is produced in saying it: the speaker's tongue makes contact with roughly the same place on the roof of his mouth in every case. Phonemes that are difficult to characterize acoustically can more easily be defined by the events of speech.[2]

These facts have been familiar for a relatively long time, but it seems to me that they have often been misinterpreted. At one point, they nearly persuaded some psychologists of a curious hypothesis called the "motor theory of speech perception."[3] According to the motor theory, we can only perceive speech by making small movements of our own tongues and other speech organs in tandem with those of the speaker, and then sensing these movements kinesthetically. How else could we know what the speaker's articulators were up to?

There are many reasons why the motor theory cannot possibly be true; I have reviewed them elsewhere[4] and there is no need to do so here. I mention it only because it represents a common misunderstanding of the view that we perceive articulatory gestures. If nothing reaches our ears except sound waves, the question runs, how could we know the movements that gave rise to them without some special imitative mechanism? To see the fallacy in this question, consider a similar visual case. No one (or at least hardly anyone) would suppose that we cannot see the motions of dancers without dancing ourselves or that we must contort our own faces to perceive another's grimace. Why should we have to move our own lips or tongues to perceive someone else's articulatory gestures? In all these cases, there are environmental events and optical or acoustical information that specifies those events. There is no reason to postulate a special mechanism when the specification is acoustic and not when it is optic. The English language is misleading in this respect: it allows us to say that we hear *sounds* when we are really hearing events, but makes it unreasonable to say that we see *light* when we are really seeing objects. Actually, the two cases are precisely analogous. We see events (or objects) by means of the information available in light, and hear them by means of the information available in sound. Although the difficult task of giving a scientific account of this information has not been solved, we must not obscure it by postulating unnecessary and mysterious acts of imitation.

The same argument also undermines another, currently more popular hypothesis. The complexity of the speech signal—the fact that there are no obvious correspondences between individual phonemes and individual chunks of the sound wave—has persuaded many theorists that speech perception is somehow unique. It is supposedly mediated by a special mechanism, or neural center, that cracks the signal's intricate code by methods unknown to the rest of the nervous system.[5] In fact, however, complex patterns of information arriving over time are the rule and not the exception in every modality. The friendliness of a gesture is "encoded" just as deeply in the changing optic array as a word is in the acoustic waveform. Speech perception is intricate, but it may not differ in principle from other kinds of perceptual activity.

It may seem far-fetched to describe speech as articulatory gesturing, and to treat speech perception as comparable to perceiving gestures of other kinds. I do not mean to deny that language is something very special. While other gestures may also have perceptible meanings, they do not form sentences or express propositions or distinguish tenses or make subtle metaphors (leaving sign language proper aside, of course). The speaker deliberately structures the events of his speech in order to express a particular meaning. If we have the appropriate schemata, we can pick up this structure quite directly, taking advantage of the several levels of organization that it exhibits. That is, we may hear both what the speaker said and what he meant. The structures of speech have their own complex rules of formation, which are the proper province of linguistics. Their complexity does not imply, however, that the act of perceiving them is radically different from the way we perceive events of other kinds.

Visual information for speech

In perceiving speech we perceive events, not just sounds. This immediately suggests the possibility that other sources of information about the events might be helpful. The fact that we can perceive speech by sound alone (as on the telephone) does not imply that other information would not be used if it were available. Indeed, it often is. Although some speech events (e.g., movements of the tongue) are concealed inside the speaker's head, others (especially lip movements) are easily visible to anyone who can see his face. Skilled lip readers can use this visual information to determine a good deal of what is said even if they are totally deaf. Interestingly enough, ordinary listeners also use it along with acoustic information when it is available; speech perception in a noisy environment improves markedly when the listener can see the speaker.[6] Although we are not usually aware of the multimodal nature of speech perception, it can become obvious in a dubbed foreign film or in a film in which picture and sound are not properly synchronized. The discovery of such an asynchrony is often disruptive. What it disrupts is the normal coherence of the information that two modalities provide about the same event.

It is interesting to note that the events of speech are accessible to still another modality—touch—if the "listener" places his hand over the speaker's lips and cheeks. This possibility is exploited in the Tadoma method of communicating with the deaf, which can provide at least some understanding of speech in the absence of both hearing and vision.[7] To perceive speech, we must pick up information that specifies articulatory gestures. Any sense modality that can accomplish this may be employed for it.

Since articulatory events are motions of certain parts of the body, speech perception has something in common with perceiving other bodily motions, like those of dancers and athletes. In particular, the perception of facial expressions, nonverbal cues, "body language," and the like must be continuous with it. There is every reason to believe that speech perception begins as just one aspect of the general perception of other people's movements and does not become sharply differentiated for a child until he realizes the denotative and propositional character of speech. Until then, the only difference is that relatively more information about speech events is carried by sound (because many speech events are inside the mouth and cannot be seen), while more information about external bodily motions is conveyed optically. I will argue in Chapter 9 that we are probably born with schemata sensitive to expressions of emotion and intention; the schemata of speech perception may develop out of such beginnings.

The case of the dubbed film is interesting for another reason. Whether or not we notice the discrepancy between the two kinds of information available, the speech we perceive is what we hear, not what we see. This is, then, an instance in which hearing *dominates* vision. The reason is obvious: the acoustic signal provides far more adequate information about speech events than does the optic array. It would certainly be otherwise for a partially deaf lip reader.

Although hearing may dominate vision in specifying articulation, the opposite is true for another important aspect of speech: its location in the environment. While people can localize sounds rather accurately when it is important to do so (primarily on the basis of time and intensity differences at the two ears), this localization is labile and easily influenced by other factors. No matter where the loudspeakers in the theater may be located, we generally tend to hear the speech as if it came from the actors portrayed on the screen. This is not so much a matter of unavoidable perceptual error (we may be able to locate the loudspeaker correctly if we make an effort to do so) as of what seems most natural.[8] Ventriloquists take advantage of this; their audiences are happy to ascribe speech to the dummy rather than to the ventriloquist because the former's mouth is in motion while the latter's is not. Sound has a way of insinuating itself into perceptual cycles where it does not actually belong, of being "referred" to events other than those that actually gave rise to it. This property may be important in the acquisition of language.

Concrete reference: a speculation

Babies like to be talked to, and luckily people like talking to them. Speech interests infants enormously, and they indicate their interest by looking at it—that is, by looking at the face of the speaker. Every movement of their mother (or anyone else) interests them: approaches, smiles, gestures, and nods as well as the movements of the articulators that we call speech. At first, they cannot know that the speech has any referential function; it is just something else that their mother is doing. They pick up all the information about it that they can with any modality available. They look at it, listen to it, may playfully put their hand up to touch it. To be sure, these activities require some initial schema to get them under way; the perceptual cycle must occur before it can develop. The specificity of the initial schemata (i.e., the degree to which human beings are innately endowed with particular capacities for speech perception) remains an open question.[9] However they may begin, these focused perceptual activities soon establish schemata specific to the patterns of articulation common in the language of the infant's home. In time he becomes able to recognize these patterns as familiar even when he can't see the speaker and must depend on acoustic information alone.

I don't really know how important the visual information is in the scenario just described. It is certainly not crucial, since blind children learn to speak. For them too, the sounds of speech must first offer information about the vocal activities of the speaker; they get less information about these activities than sighted children do, but they seem to manage. (There would be little point in comparing the ages of speech onset in blind and sighted children, since parents surely talk to the former more often, or at least differently, than the latter). The main point here is not that there is a visual contribution to intelligibility, but that every child attends to a good deal of speech before he has any idea that it refers to objects and events other than itself. In this way he develops perceptual schemata that can detect linguistic differences and anticipate linguistic structures.

Infants do not merely listen to speech sounds; they also try to make them. They are not very successful in the beginning, but they persevere. Even before they

succeed in imitating anyone else's noises, they make
plenty of their own. Making sounds is probably just as
interesting to them as looking at objects. Indeed, from a
certain point of view, the two activities are quite similar. In both cases the perceiver engages in certain muscular movements and adjustments, with the result that
certain kinds of information become available to him. In
vocalizing, the movements are those of his articulators,
and what they produce is new auditory information. In
seeing, the movements are those of his head and eyes,
and what they "produce" (make available) is new optical information. This structural similarity may make it
easy to incorporate articulatory activity into the perceptual cycle when naming begins.

If infants were interested only in articulatory
events—other people's or their own—they would never
learn to talk. But they are fascinated by nearly everything else in their environment as well: toys and food
and pets and people, games and repetitions, comings
and goings. (As has been pointed out many times, they
could not possibly acquire language about such things
unless they could perceive them first.[10]) Let us imagine,
then, a baby who is attending to some object or event. It
will often happen that his mother is attending to it too;
mothers are generally interested in what their babies
are doing, and babies in turn frequently follow their
mothers' line of regard.[11] In many cases, she will not
only attend to the focal object but say the appropriate
word: "Doggie," perhaps. What is the child to make of
the acoustic information he is thus offered?

At such a moment, the lucky infant is engaged in two
perceptual cycles at once. He is picking up information
about his mother (she is speaking) and about the dog (it
has just come into the room). He is, we may assume,

temporarily more interested in the dog. The new information is acoustic, which means that it can be rather freely appropriated by any ongoing perceptual cycle. What is more natural than that he comes to treat the sound as some sort of attribute of the dog? To be sure, it is not a consistently available attribute; no one says "doggie" like clockwork whenever the creature appears. But this is not an unusual state of affairs, since most attributes of objects are only sporadically available. We cannot see a dog's tail all the time, nor continuously hear its bark, yet these irregularities do not prevent us from treating both as the animal's inalienable possessions. In this way the *names* of objects—the words most frequently used to denote them—become incorporated into the anticipatory schemata by which the objects themselves are perceived.[12]

The suggestion I am making is not a new one. Others have proposed that young children treat the names of objects as if they were intrinsic properties.[13] Without some such hypothesis, I think it would be impossible to explain how words come to refer to objects at all (and indeed, the hypothesis is little more than a restatement of that fact). Nevertheless, it must not be taken too literally. The name belongs to the object only in a special sense; the child knows perfectly well that "doggie" is not hung around the dog's neck or concealed in its fur. In fact, he knows that it was something *said by his mother;* he has long since developed perceptual schemata that automatically pick up this information. A name is a property of a thing which must be uttered by a person; its charm and its power lie precisely in the confluence of these two perceptual cycles. Words specify their referents as well as the articulatory gestures of the speaker.

The fact that words are sounds, and thus less closely tied to their actual sources than other signs would be, probably makes it easier to incorporate them in these dual schemata. A child can localize them at their real origin in his mother's face if he wants to, just as we can listen for the location of the loudspeaker in the theater, but it is also easy for him to treat them as belonging to the objects of attention. A visual signal, such as a gesture in sign language, might not have this advantage. The child would be naturally inclined to treat it just as something his mother was doing, rather than as somehow connected with the signified object. Of course it is possible for people (or chimpanzees) to learn various kinds of sign-language, but they must be *taught*. The contingencies must be deliberately arranged, at least at first. (For example the mother of a deaf child may carefully make the sign for cookie as her signing hand touches the cookie itself.) I do not think language would have evolved spontaneously among organisms that could not hear.

Let us now consider how the names of things can come to elicit images of them in their absence. Perceiving the dog (or anything) takes time; it involves schematic anticipation as well as information pickup. This means that the dog's name is not simply associated to some momentary sense impression, but embedded in a schema. It becomes part of what the child is ready for whenever any information about the dog has become available. Conversely he comes to anticipate seeing the dog, and actively searches for it, whenever he hears its name. Later on, the process of detachment will begin: the word *doggie* will create a visual readiness even when he knows that the dog is nowhere nearby and is not really to be expected. Thus the names of things become able to evoke images of them, with incalculable consequences.

People do not generally speak in isolated words, of course; almost no one does except in conversing with infants. We talk in sentences whose meanings depend on their grammatical organization as well as on the words they include. Isolated words really have no meaning at all, except when some perceptible context plays the role that sentences usually perform. There are many competing linguistic accounts of sentence structure. I cannot review them here, though it is worth noting that some of the recent accounts offer grammatical descriptions modeled after the structure of natural events: they include agents, actions, locations, and similar theoretical categories.[14] It has been suggested that this makes it relatively easy for children to understand sentences, to "see what they mean." Since one invariably speaks to infants about events in their immediate environment, they can see the referent concretely as they hear the sentence, and the two schemata can become interrelated. In some such way as this, not yet well understood, infants come to understand sentences as well as single words.

Sentences take time to utter and to hear. The perceptual cycle that links the listener to the articulatory gestures of the speaker often lasts for many seconds, and anticipations generated at the beginning may not be satisfied until the end. I suppose that a principal function of grammatical structure must be to help the listener span this time, so he can develop anticipations in units larger than the articulatory gestures. The presence of the referent events themselves can also serve this purpose, of course, but adults do not always talk about nearby objects. Without grammar, lengthy utterances about remote events would hardly be comprehensible at all. Skilled speakers (and writers) are aware of this, and arrange the structure of their sentences so that their listeners (or readers) can keep track of them.

The origins of introspection

If mental images are perceptual anticipations, a description of a visual image is a description of what one is ready to see. To really understand how this might be possible, we would have to begin by understanding what seems to be a simpler problem: how does one describe what one *does* see? Unfortunately, even this is still too difficult in the present state of linguistic theory. Although substantial progress has been made in recent years, the problem has not been clarified enough to permit a detailed treatment here. Consequently, the present speculation will not go much beyond the one-word descriptions, or names, that have already been considered. How does a child come to name things?

We have already seen that making sounds is in many respects analogous to perceiving. Both activities involve doing things to make information available. If there is a dog in the room, a child can make visual information about it available by moving his head and eyes; he can make acoustic information about it (the word *doggie*) appear by moving his articulators. Of course, he must first find out how to do this. As in the case of listening to speech, it is unclear how much innate equipment this discovery requires. It certainly requires having articulators in the first place, and some specific neural apparatus to control them is probably necessary as well.

However it may begin, every normal child eventually discovers that he can make speech sounds and say words himself. He immediately starts to do so in the contexts in which these words are appropriate, that is, in the presence of the objects they name. Because the two schemata are already linked, saying "doggie" may seem to him much like the other exploratory movements he makes to bring new properties of the dog into view. To be sure, the two contingencies are actually quite different. The optical information he gets by looking depends intrinsically on the real attributes of the dog; it specifies those attributes by virtue of the laws of optics. The acoustic information he gets by speaking is linked to its referent more tenuously; it specifies the dog only by linguistic convention. The child probably has some inkling of this from the beginning, since he knows that verbal sounds specify speech events as well as objects. Nevertheless, there must be a stage in development when naming things is deeply embedded in the very process of perceiving them. The schema of the object includes subschemata for vocalization as well as for visual exploration, and it motivates both activities at once.

The same principle can be applied to other early uses of words. Children don't just say things like "doggie." They use one-word utterances for many purposes besides naming: consider, for example, "hi" and "no." Some of these usages are embedded in schemata for perceiving *events* rather than objects. Saying "hi," for example, is a part of the (perceptual) activity of seeing someone enter the room. Others are embedded in what seem to be schemata for action rather than perception: "no" is part of refusing something, along with struggling or turning away. In every case, the spoken word begins as an integral part of some larger, cyclical activity. Only later does it become detached from that activity and enlisted in the service of other schemata.

If naming an object is embedded in the schema with which that object is perceived, it must be involved in the process of *imagining* the object as well. Mental images are perceptual anticipations: schemata active independently of the perceptual cycle to which they would normally pertain. If such a schema includes plans for speaking as well as plans for looking, the image may be accompanied by speech. Thus a young child who forms an image of the dog for some reason—perhaps because he heard it bark—is quite likely to say "dog" as he does so. Although he does not know it yet, he is describing his image. That is, he is talking about what he merely imagines, in a way which would be appropriate if he were really seeing it. Later he will say more complicated things in connection with his images, and psychologists will credit him with the ability to introspect.

A one-word description is not much, of course. Children soon learn to talk in sentences; their "mean length of utterance," as it is called, does not remain indefinitely at a value of one. Because we really do not know how sentences are put together to refer to events, I cannot say how they describe anticipations of events either. It is clear, though, that sentences involve extended anticipations in their own right. "Plans for speaking," as Miller, Galanter and Pribram called them some time ago,[15] are long and complex. Like plans for looking, they are rarely specific in advance. We "know what we are going to say" before saying it, but only in the rather general way that we know what we are going to see before seeing it. When we know it well, we can make minor changes from one occasion to the next without disturbing the overall structure, just as we can incorporate new information into cognitive maps. That is why sentences, too, are effective mnemonic devices.

At first, the child can only talk about things that he is actually perceiving and doing or that he anticipates in the immediate future. Perceptual schemata are firmly anchored to available information, and so are words. Later in development he learns to break the perceptual cycle, detaching his anticipations from the stimulus information that originally instigated and confirmed them, and enlisting them in other schemata for other reasons. He acquires the adult ability to anticipate things perceptually without really expecting them at all; i.e., to imagine what he knows will not really happen. It is not surprising that he manages to describe these quasi-anticipated events; he is already skilled in describing more realistically anticipated ones. The describing and the imagining are concurrent. Because each is extended in time, it is hopeless to try to determine which starts earlier, as some psychologists have done.[16] Neither occurs at a single definable instant, and neither is in any simple way the cause of the other.

This ability to talk about imagined events is the origin of the "displacement" that Hockett has defined as one of the critical properties of language.[17] It cannot happen in speech until it has happened in perception; that is, we cannot talk about remote events until we can imagine them. On the other hand, there is no reason why it should lag far behind. If children succeed in decontextualizing and manipulating their images only after they have learned to talk, imagination and introspective description may well appear at the same moment in development. It is by no means easy to detach them from each other even intentionally. Children are notoriously poor liars; the ability to think one thing and say another is a late-developing skill.

Among psychologists, and for many adults, the term *introspection* carries mysterious overtones. We seem to be describing something that is inside us rather than in our environment, something examinable only by the mind's eye and not by the body's. Children do not have these hang-ups. Even when they are giving fluent descriptions of things they cannot see, they do not think of themselves as engaged in self-report. Consider this conversation with a five-year-old, taken from a recent study of cognitive maps in children:

E: Pretend that your mom is calling you down to the kitchen and you're up in your bedroom. Can you tell me how you would get from your bedroom to the kitchen?

S: O.K., you open (the) door and then you have a stairs going down.

E: Oh, is the stairway right by your room? Or do you have to go past some other rooms before you get to the stairway?

S: No, we have to go past two storage rooms.

E: Two storage rooms. O.K., and then you go down the stairway, huh? What do you do when you get to the bottom of the stairway?

S: Then I can turn that way or that way.

E: What if you turn over there; where do you go?

S: That will go to the bathroom or my mom's room or in the den.

E: Oh, how do you get to the kitchen then when you get to the bottom of the stairs?

S: Oh, well you just turn that way.

E: That way? And then do you have to go through

> another room before you get to the kitchen? Is
> the kitchen right there?
>
> S: You just turn that way and just go straight and
> then you'll see the stove and the sink.[18]

This subject has a well-developed cognitive map of
his house and can accurately anticipate what he would
see from various station points. In the interview, he is
deploying these anticipations in a detached, counterfactual way, and accompanying them with appropriate
language. Nevertheless, it would not be fair to say that
he was "describing his cognitive map" to the experimenter; he would not have understood such an introspectively worded instruction at all. He was talking
about a house, not a mental state. Five-year-olds have
not yet absorbed the dualistic metaphysics according to
which images are ghostly internal entities, observable
in their own right. In this respect they may be wiser
than we are. What seem to us like descriptions of images and cognitive maps are really—that is, logically
and developmentally—descriptions of potentially perceivable objects, of what one would see if such-and-
such a thing were present. Introspection is a kind of
preparation for exterospection.

Notes

1. This fact has often been documented; see Liberman,
   Cooper, Shankweiler, and Studdert-Kennedy (1967). It
   has recently been challenged by Cole and Scott (1974[a],
   [b]), but their evidence does not invalidate the position
   taken here.
2. I do not mean that every phoneme corresponds to exactly

one position of the articulators. Some are represented by several distinct positions (/g/ is articulated differently in /gi/ and /gu/, for example); in such cases the different positions could and often do function as separate phonemes in other languages. Moreover, the movements of the articulators that constitute a given phoneme are not quite the same in all contexts; they vary according to the preceding and following phoneme. These coarticulation effects are analogous to the flexibility of detail in other, more obvious gestures. (A friendly wave of your hand is executed one way if you are just taking your hand from your pocket and another if you have just been scratching your ear.) Difficult problems of definition remain in all these cases. The present argument suggests only that the best way to approach them is in terms of the articulatory gestures, where they are no different in principle from the general problems of event perception.

3. Liberman (1957).

4. Neisser (1967).

5. This hypothesis was originally presented by Liberman et al. (1967), and is now widely accepted. One piece of evidence frequently advanced to support it is that a particular region in the dominant hemisphere of the brain, the *speech area*, is critically involved in speaking and listening. Destruction of this area produces aphasia; disconnection of the two hemispheres makes people unable to speak about visual information presented to the nondominant one; speech presented to the contralateral ear (which has privileged connections to the dominant hemisphere) has various advantages over speech presented to the other ear, and so on. These observations show that the speech area has indeed become specialized for speech. They do not prove, however, that what it does is fundamentally different from what happens elsewhere in the brain.

6. Sumby and Pollack (1954).

7. Alcorn (1945).

8. Actually a certain amount of error may be unavoidable in such cases: several experiments have shown that the per-

ceived directions of sound sources in a dark room are attracted toward visible points of light. See also recent work by Thurlow and Jack (1973; Jack and Thurlow, 1973) on ventriloquism, which shows that the effect depends critically on the time relations between the visual and auditory patterns.

9. Studies of "phoneme detection" in infants suggest that the schemata critical for speech are present very early and probably have a genetic basis (Eimas, Siqueland, Jusczyk, and Vigorito, 1971). An infant who has been sucking on a nipple to produce the spoken sound of a particular syllable (the contingency is electronically arranged) will gradually stop responding; i.e. he will "habituate." The evidence for phoneme detection is his renewed responsiveness when a phoneme in the syllable is altered; this dishabituation is less marked if the syllable is changed in a manner that does not cross phoneme boundaries. But very recent studies have found similar evidence for phoneme detection in animals as well (Kuhl and Miller, 1975; Waters and Wilson, 1976). This is not surprising if phonemes are perceivable articulatory events. All animals must have schemata for event perception, especially for the characteristic movements of other animals. (This point will be considered further in Chapter 9.) The schemata used in speech perception may develop from more fundamental ones that are already prepared to pick up information differentiating one event from another.

10. MacNamara (1972) is among those who have recently made this point, and it is central to Nelson's (1974) theory of language acquisition.

11. Bruner (1975) cites evidence on this point.

12. The term *name* is not really appropriate, although no better word seems to be available. Fodor, Bever, and Garrett (1974) point out that common nouns like "dog" are *not* names: they have meaning, whereas names merely specify particular objects. One might ask what *dog* means but it makes no sense to ask what *Fido* means.

13. For example Vygotsky, who points out how confused children become if you suggest to them that things might

have other names than they actually do. "When asked whether one could interchange the names of objects, for instance call a cow 'ink' and ink 'cow,' the child will answer no, 'because ink is used for writing and the cow gives milk.' An exchange of names would mean an exchange of characteristic features, so inseparable is the connection between them in the child's mind." (1962, p. 129).

14. For an introduction to these grammars and their possible uses, see MacNamara (1972), Brown (1973), and Bruner (1975). A recent article by Luria (1975) stresses the importance of explaining the acquisition of language in terms of other basic processes including perception and action; his view is very close to the one proposed here.

15. Miller, Galanter, and Pribram (1960).

16. See, for example, Paivio (1971, pp. 441–444).

17. Hockett (1960).

18. Pick (1972), pp. 1–2.

Some Consequences of Cognition

It is often argued that progress in psychology represents a danger to personal liberty. If psychology is a science, its goal must be to understand general principles of human nature. Armed with these principles, will it not be able to control the objects of its study? Many people take this possibility seriously, and not all of them view it with alarm. B. F. Skinner, for example, has repeatedly suggested that adequate methods of behavioral control are already available and could improve the human condition tomorrow if we were not too timid to put them into practice.[1] It seems to me, however, that both the hopes and the fears which accompany the notion of behavioral control are misplaced. The facts of cognition imply that the psychological manipulation of behavior is bound to fail; it cannot lead to systematically predictable outcomes under ordinary cultural conditions.

This is not to say that behavior cannot be predicted or manipulated. We all engage in a great deal of prediction every day, and usually in a little manipulation as well. Society could hardly exist if we did not. Moreover, everyone is familiar with cases in which one person has manipulated another, or even a great many others, in his own interest. The fact that manipulations sometimes succeed, however, does not prove that they would succeed oftener if the manipulators knew more psychology; the scope of behavioral control may have intrinsic limits. This possibility deserves a close examination.

Choosing where to look and what to do

Before deciding whether behavior can be controlled by psychological means, we must consider how it is controlled ordinarily; i.e., what it depends on. Attempts to answer this question have too often been over-simplified. They are usually based on the assumption that there are only two possibilities: either the individual himself determines what he will see and do (he is *free*), or else his environment determines it (he is *controlled*). Where the control of perceptual activity is concerned, two solutions are currently popular among cognitive psychologists. The first, considered in Chapter 5, distinguishes sharply between perception and attention. Perception proper is thought to be determined by impinging stimuli, while a mechanism of selective attention remains under the control of the individual himself. We have already seen that this proposal will not do; selectivity is inherent in the very process of information pickup and cannot be relegated to any separate device. The second, which must be considered here, is due to J. S. Bruner.[2] He assigns control to the perceiver, who is said to go increasingly far "beyond the information given' as he acquires more sophisticated perceptual skills. In this view, the main thrust of cognitive development is to make the adult freer than the child: he is said to be less "stimulus-bound" and more "inner-directed." In their study of eye movements, for example, Mackworth and Bruner suggest that "visual search must develop from a state in which the gaze is controlled by the nature of the stimulus and its intrinsic features to one in which it is, in the words of Yarbus, an instrument of thought."[3] In the same vein, Eleanor J. Gibson says that attention "changes from being captured to being exploratory" and quotes William James's comment that "[the] reflex and passive character of the [child's] attention, which . . . makes the child seem less to belong to himself than to every object which happens to catch his notice, is the first thing the teacher must overcome."[4]

The notion that adults are freer and less controlled by their environment than children, better able to go beyond the information given, points to something important about maturity and freedom. In its usual formulation, however, it cannot be right. Children are spontaneous, unpredictable, and free of convention; how can they also be stimulus-bound? In the very paper from which the foregoing quotation was drawn, Mackworth and Bruner found that the eye movement patterns of their adult subjects were more conventional (i.e., more similar to one another given the same picture) than those of the children! It is odd, then, to describe them as less controlled.

This paradox appears in all areas of perception and behavior. To understand it, let us consider a different, nondevelopmental example of the relation between perception and the environment: the game of chess.

One of the characteristics of a good chess player is his skill in picking up relevant information from the board. This is obvious not only from the success of his play, but also from various indirect measures. A master can reproduce the entire position on the board after a five-second look at it, for example; no amateur player can do nearly as well. The master succeeds because he can perceive certain aspects of the position that escape a lesser player; structural characteristics that, once seen, constrain the locations of the pieces themselves very precisely. Experience has endowed him with a great many schemata for recurring constellations of pieces; Chase and Simon[5] estimate that an expert player may have a vocabulary of schematic constellations about as large as most people's vocabulary of words.

The information that the master picks up from the chessboard determines not only where he will move his pieces but where he will move his eyes. Observations show that a good chess player's eye movements are closely related to the structure of the position on the board; he looks at crucial pieces and crucial squares.[6] He quite literally *sees* the position differently—more adequately and comprehensively—than a novice or a nonplayer would. Of course, even the nonplayer sees a great deal: the chessmen are of carved ivory, the knight resembles a horse, the pieces are (perhaps) arrayed with a certain geometrical regularity. A young child would see still less: that the pieces would fit in his mouth, perhaps, or could be knocked over. A newborn infant might just see that "something" was in front of him. To be sure, he is not mistaken in this; something *is* in front of him. The differences among these perceivers are not matters of truth and error but of noticing more rather than less. The information that specifies the proper move is as available in the light sampled by the baby as by the master, but only the master is equipped to pick it up.

Although the optic array specifies the available moves and their consequences as well as the physical properties of the pieces, the principles underlying these two kinds of specification are very different. As noted in Chapter 4, light carries information about the layout of the environment simply by virtue of the laws of optics. Its specification of possible moves, however, is established by the rules of chess, which are essentially a social convention. The distinction is analogous to the one considered earlier for the sounds of speech. "Doggie" refers to dogs by linguistic convention, while it specifies the articulatory gestures of the speaker for inevitable acoustic reasons. Perceivers do not go beyond the information given, but cultures go beyond the elementary contingencies of nature to make additional information available. The rules of chess do not control the master's perception; they make it possible by giving him something to perceive.

Such an interpretation suggests that the chess player is neither totally free to look and move where he chooses nor entirely at the mercy of his environment. The control of eye movements and all adaptive behavior is only comprehensible as an interaction. The schema directs eye movements that pick up information that modifies the schema that directs further movements. Any particular motion is "caused" by the entire history of the cycle in which it lies. To be sure, its most immediate cause is the schema itself: a momentary state of the perceiver's nervous system. This is just as true for the infant's reflexive look toward a sudden sound as the chess master's thoughtful glance toward his opponent's queen. But since the state of each schema is partly determined by stimulus information accepted earlier, both eye movements are at least partly governed by (i.e., appropriate to) their respective situations.

The same principle applies to the development of all skilled perception. Perceptual cycles vary in the kind and scope of the information that guides them. Unsophisticated perceivers are tuned to relatively superficial features of their environment; skilled perceivers to subtler ones. The adult is more future oriented and more effectively goal directed than the child, but not more independent of the world around him. Perceiving is a matter of picking up information, not of going beyond it.

Choosing where to look is not the same thing as choosing what to do. When we select one *action* rather than another, the embedding schema usually includes some anticipation of our own future situation; like a cognitive map, it contains the ego. We expect to be pleased with ourselves, or rewarded, or at least content, if we choose A; we may expect little good to come of B. Perceptual choices seem less momentous than these and are usually made with little reference to such outcomes. Despite this difference, however, perceptual and behavioral choices have the same existential status. No choice is ever free of the information on which it is based. Nevertheless, that information is selected by the chooser himself. On the other hand, no choice is ever determined by the environment directly. Still, that environment supplies the information that the chooser will use.

The limitations of prediction and control

The foregoing argument implies that the prediction and control of behavior is not primarily a psychological matter. What would we have to know to predict how a chess master will move his pieces, or his eyes? His moves are based on information he has picked up from the board, so they can only be predicted by someone who has access to the same information. In other words, an aspiring predictor would have to understand the position at least as well as the master does; he would have to be a chessmaster himself! If I play chess against a master he will always win, precisely because he can predict and control my behavior while I cannot do the reverse. To change this situation I must improve my knowledge of chess, not of psychology.

Note that the chessmaster does not control my behavior by any psychological device.[7] He simply makes legal moves, which have the effect of changing my environment and the possibilities it offers. Indeed, this is almost always how behavior is controlled. Changing the world is a very powerful way of changing behavior; changing the individual while leaving the world alone is a dubious proposition. And no change can have "controlling," or predictable, results unless the relevant sector of the world is well understood.

Chess is a rather esoteric skill, but the point applies generally. Because perception and action take place in continuous dependence on the environment, they cannot be understood without an understanding of that environment itself. This means that the psychologist cannot predict and control anyone who knows more about the situation than he does, or who picks up information that he has left out of the reckoning. But the human environment is vastly complicated, and a huge array of disciplines from political science to traffic engineering has sprung up in the effort to understand it. Few of these disciplines can claim any great success to date, but my purpose here is not to criticize them. It is to urge a measure of humility on the discipline that calls itself "behavioral science." The prediction and control of behavior in the real world requires detailed knowledge of that world to a degree that we usually do not have, and that in any case falls outside the realm of psychological expertise.

This analysis not only suggests that absolute control would be out of the question without a complete understanding of the environment, but also indicates the conditions under which some degree of control is possible. Tightly controlled environments—prisoner-of-war camps, penal institutions, mental hospitals, and the like—often manage to control their inmates fairly well. (Even in these situations, an impressive and heartening number of people find ways to maintain their individuality.) It is chiefly in such environments that the various popularly feared (or advocated) methods of control, from brainwashing to behavior modification, have been successful. Their successes should not be taken as proof of any particular psychological theory, however; they only show that people can behave adaptively in situations that offer few alternatives. More important, there is little evidence that any manipulation undertaken in these environments has predictable consequences after the subject's release. Incarceration can have powerful and continuing effects, of course, but the particular behavior that will result from it cannot be foreseen.

There is another consequence of the argument. Control of behavior requires not only a relatively closed environment but also one that the controller understands at least as well as the controllee and preferably better. This is one of the initial advantages that parents have over their children; their control is weakened (for better or for worse) as soon as the child enters new environments that they do not know much about. More generally, everything that a person learns makes him less susceptible to control. People with knowledge are necessarily harder to manipulate than those who lack it, for the same reason that skilled chess players are harder to beat than duffers. Truth does make us free. Real education is not primarily a technique for manipulating students, as some have suggested, but just the opposite. This isn't because schooling makes people rebellious, but because it enables them to see more possibilities for action.

So far, my argument for the impracticability of behavioral control has dealt only with perception and action. I have not mentioned imagination, abstraction, or speech. Since these achievements are based on the detachment of cognitive processes from the individual's immediate situation, however, they are necessarily even harder to predict or control. Images are readinesses for information that the environment does not actually offer, and speech begins as an incomplete perceptual activity. Any attempt to manipulate such detached activities seems doomed to failure at the outset. This may seem unimportant in some contexts, since a would-be manipulator might be satisfied to control what people do while ignoring what they say and think. In the long run, however, we know that images and ideas can have powerful and unexpected consequences for action.

Before leaving this topic, it may be useful to reiterate that real manipulation occurs all the time without benefit of psychological theory. One of the most effective manipulatory techniques even follows from the present argument. Since behavior is based on information, it can be affected by misinformation. Lying is hardly a discovery of psychologists, but it often works. The only defense against it is to maintain available sources of information that the liar does not control. The connection between freedom of choice and access to valid information is fundamental; one cannot meaningfully exist without the other. This poses a particularly acute danger to freedom in contemporary society, in which various kinds of middlemen and media control our access to important facts. The supposed threat to liberty posed by sinister manipulative psychologists is an illusion, but the danger of being systematically misinformed is very real.

Social prediction

The argument so far suggests that no one—not even a psychologist armed with a good theory—can be sure what another person will do in an incompletely understood situation. Even when the situation is clear, however, another difficulty remains. Since perception and behavior are controlled interactively, their course depends on the individual as well as the environment; a predictor would have to understand the former as well as the latter. That is, one must know another person's schemata and intentions to know what he will do. This is necessarily difficult, since these schemata are locked inscrutably within his skull where we cannot see them. What kinds of information might help to specify their nature?

Any consideration of this problem must begin with the fact that we *do* predict one another's behavior, with consistency and success, in many of the encounters of ordinary life. We can anticipate people's reactions to physical objects like chairs and doors and telephones; we comfortably assume their compliance with cultural norms like driving on the right and wearing clothes; we see that they are happy or angry or afraid, and accurately predict the occurrence of emotional behavior. These predictions can be made with confidence only in more or less familiar situations, but they are not less interesting on that account.

At first glance, the account of cognition given in this book only seems to make the matter more mysterious. Schemata are developed by experience; everyone's experiences are different; therefore we must all be very different from one another. Since every person's perceptual history is unique we should all have unique cognitive structures, and the differences between us can only increase as we grow older and become more individualized. Indeed, we did not even start out alike: unless you are an identical twin, you were born different from anyone else who ever lived. While not much is known about *how* genetic differences affect behavior (despite all the politically loaded essays on the subject), it is clear *that* they affect behavior. Infants are differently active, mobile, and responsive from birth; it is more than likely that they start with different perceptual schemata as well.

This is true as far as it goes, and it poses another formidable obstacle to the fine-grained prediction of perception or behavior. Nevertheless, it overstates the case. We all do see the chessboard, even if we overlook the mating combination; we all perceive the same gross features of the environment, even if we disagree about their affordances. Such congruence must mean that the worlds we have lived in are not so different after all, and that our initial schemata equipped each of us to notice some of the same things.

Everyone lives in a world of objects: things with surfaces, usually opaque, resistant to the touch, rigid, often but not always movable, of various colors, and so on. Information specifying such properties is available to any organism with schemata to accept it. Since this information has great adaptive significance—survival is hardly possible without it, at least for large animals—it is not surprising that we have these schemata. All of us see the chessboard because (a) there is information available that specifies its physical properties; (b) we began life with schemata tuned at least roughly to properties of this sort; (c) our extensive experience with objects (if not with chessboards) has developed these schemata to a point where such information can be picked up quickly and accurately.

Our shared experience does not include only the physical environment. To the extent that we live in a coherent culture, we have encountered a more or less standardized set of social experiences as well. We expect people to drive on the right (and talk sense and sleep at night and eat three meals a day when they can) because we have often seen it done before. We develop anticipations of common behavior in the same way that we develop anticipations of other events, and we perceive them in the same cyclic way. These culturally established schemata mediate our perception of other people's behavior, and also underlie that behavior itself. They reflect just the level of predictability that culture requires and creates: not enough to tell anyone's fortune, but enough to get through the day.

Emotion and physiognomic perception

One other kind of person perception remains to be considered. We do not see other people only as generalized members of society, but as individuals with changing emotions and feelings. They approach us with hostile or friendly intent, look frightened or cheerful or angry. As noted in an earlier chapter, such physiognomic traits are perceived more easily than the physical movements that give evidence of them. I can literally see how you feel.

A number of special hypothesis have been advanced to explain this kind of perception, but none is very satisfactory. Do we first see the movements, gestures, and expressions themselves, and then infer their meaning on the basis of past occasions when we saw similar ones? Surely not. The process is too quick and automatic, appears too early in childhood, is too independent of reasoning and inferential ability. Does the sight of an emotional person arouse identical feelings in us by some mysterious empathy—feelings that we then ingeniously assign to the perceived person rather than to ourselves? This notion creates more problems than it solves. A perceptual theory is still required to explain how we get the necessary information in the first place, and it must be supplemented by some account of how we detect our own inner feelings and why we attribute them to another. Besides, it does not ring true: surely we can perceive hostility without being hostile or passion without being impassioned. The empathy theory has the same logical form as the motor theory of speech perception, and suffers from essentially the same defects.

The simplest approach to this problem is to suppose that physiognomic perception is no different from any other kind. It requires a preparatory schema, ready to pick up information and to direct explorations that will pick up still more. As in ordinary perceiving, this information specifies something that really exists. In the physiognomic case, that "something" is another person's emotion or feeling. How can such states be perceivable? I believe it is because they are themselves anticipations, at least in part. Anger is the inner aspect of anticipated aggression, in the same sense that an image is the inner aspect of a perceptual schema. In a sense, it is an intention. It can be detached from the circumstances in which the aggression would actually occur, just as an image can be detached from the perceptual cycle. In both cases, however, detachment requires a considerable degree of cognitive maturity.

This explanation implies more than a hypothesis[8] about the nature of emotion. It makes two further assumptions as well. First, people must actually offer information to signal their intentions; second, the perceiver must have schemata to pick this information up. Neither of these assumptions is particularly radical. Ethologists have found anticipatory signaling behavior, and appropriate responsiveness to it, in every corner of the animal kingdom. Fish indicate their readiness for mating or combat by changing their color or posture or activity; their conspecifics react appropriately. Mammals, too, adopt certain standardized postures when they are prepared to fight and others when they intend to submit. Their attitudes give their fellows visible evidence of what they are going to do, and it is used. Neither the behavioral signals nor the responses are as highly stereotyped as has sometimes been suggested, but there is no doubt of their importance.

I am assuming, then, that we all have schemata for physiognomic perception. Such schemata could not appear out of nowhere, and it is not easy to imagine how they might develop from nonsocial experiences. It seems likely that their origin is innate. Like other animals, we are born somewhat ready to pick up the expressive signals offered by members of our own species. Babies are innately prepared to perceive smiles or frowns, soothing tones or harsh inflections, as indications of what significant others will do next.[9] Of course, this does not mean that our emotional lives consist of automatic responses to triggering stimuli, or that psychology will be made obsolete by progress in genetics.[10] Schemata for action and for physiognomic perception undergo as much development as any other cognitive structures; indeed, they are particularly dependent on social experience. Feelings are no more predictable than images or actions.

It seems to me that the development of physiognomic perception must be more idiosyncratic and individual than the development of object or event perception. A harsh tone in a parent's voice may have signalled one intention in A's family, but a very different thing in B's. Our experiences with other persons diverge much more widely than our experiences with inanimate things. As a result, there are wide differences in physiognomic perception; two people who have both been watching the same third person may disagree sharply about what he meant or how he felt.

Identity and communication

We do not perceive only other people, but also ourselves. As far as our physical properties and motions are concerned, this poses no special theoretical problems. As pointed out in Chapter 6, every mobile organism has access to a great deal of information that specifies his own position and motion. The flow patterns in the visual field alone are enough to indicate how he is moving in the environment, and one or another part of his own body is almost constantly in his field of view. No other object can possibly be confused with the self, and no other event offers the same information as a self-initiated one. Some psychologists have suggested that infants make mistakes in such matters, and cannot (for example) distinguish their mothers from themselves. I think that this hypothesis must be wrong; the difference is plainly visible.

Although the physical ego is perceivable from the beginning, the personal ego may not enjoy this advantage. An infant can see *where* he is (in relation to nearby objects), but he cannot see *who* he is or *what* he is. When he moves he can see where he is going, but not what he intends to do. If the assumption of innately based physiognomic schemata is correct, he probably perceives that his parents and his brothers and sisters are persons who have intentions and feelings long before he discovers that he is one as well. Their faces are visible while his is not. He cannot yet imagine his own actions in any but the most immediate future; the ability to detach images from their contexts matures only slowly. Who is he?

It seems likely that learning about oneself takes a long time. As many psychologists have suggested, self-knowledge is probably dependent on other-knowledge; self-perception requires the schemata that physiognomic perception first develops. A child eventually comes to anticipate his own actions and think of himself as a particular kind of person, but only with the aid of socially-developed conceptions of what a person might be. As continued cycles of anticipation and confirmation slowly establish the terms of his existence, he quite literally becomes somebody in his own eyes.

He has a lot to learn. He must find his way in the human world as well as the geographical one: anticipate the consequences of social as well as perceptual exploration. These two kinds of exploration have much in common. The geographical environment offers a rich texture of information to the exploring eye, and the perceiver becomes attuned to it by carrying out perceptual activity over time. Locomotion in that environment requires information pickup if it is to be successful, but also provides the mover with more information than he could ever obtain by remaining at rest. In particular, it specifies his own movements and characteristics as well as those of his world. In the course of mastering it, he acquires a complex and versatile cognitive structure he can use for many other purposes.

The social environment is, in a sense, even richer. It is an elaboration of possibilities that the natural world affords, constructed in the course of cultural history and through history of the individual's own family and social group. One can discover much about it as a relatively passive observer, but there is much more that can be discovered only through action. And social action, like simple locomotion, informs us about ourselves as well as about the world with which we are engaged. It, too, creates cognitive structures that have many other uses.

Much of what we need to know about society and other people and ourselves can be learned only at second hand. As social beings, we depend on what others say (or write) for information about everything that we cannot observe directly: remote events, enduring personal dispositions, or hypothesized cognitive structures. Such information is adequate for many purposes, but it is never complete no matter how effectively or skillfully it may be presented. Human communication offers unparalleled opportunities for understanding, but also for error, misunderstanding, and deceit. Our dependence on it means that our understanding of one another and ourselves—or even of subjects like cognitive psychology—is never complete and often simply mistaken. On the other hand, the perceptual cycle tends to be self-correcting, and there is always more information available than has yet been used. The outcome of any single encounter between cognition and reality is unpredictable, but in the long run such encounters must move us closer to the truth.

Notes

1. Skinner's most recent discussion of his views appears in *Beyond Freedom and Dignity* (1971), but he has made the same point often before. For a useful collection of opposing arguments on this subject, see Bever and Terrace (1973).
2. Bruner (1957, 1973).
3. Mackworth and Bruner (1970, p. 166).
4. E. J. Gibson (1969, p. 456).
5. Chase and Simon (1973); Simon and Chase (1973).
6. Simon and Barenfeld (1969).
7. Chess players sometimes play "psychologically;" that is, they take account of their opponent's temperament or his habits of play as well as of the position on the board. But this is only a marginally useful strategy; it will not help a duffer beat an expert, and it cannot be relied on in weak positions.

8. The hypothesis is not particularly original. Note, however, that it is quite different from the James-Lange theory of emotions. We do not become afraid because we run away, as that theory suggested; indeed, running away may *reduce* fear, just as actual aggression reduces or eliminates anger at least temporarily. The emotions I am considering here (which are not intended to exhaust the possible range of human feelings, of course) are connected with the anticipation of behavior rather than its execution.

9. Certain kinds of pathology, especially infantile autism, may be due to a congenital inadequacy of these schemata.

10. The exaggerated claims of certain biologists, such as E. O. Wilson (1975), have recently confused this issue to an unfortunate extent. The fact that human cognitive structure has a genetic basis does not make behavior predictable, nor can it be used to deduce any ultimate moral standards. Behavior, like perception, is a continuing interaction with the social and natural environment. It can be understood only with respect to that environment, whose historically-developed characteristics lie as far outside the scope of sociobiology as of behavioral science. Neither biology nor any other science will relieve us of the responsibility of making our own decisions.

Bibliography

Acredolo, L. P., Pick, H. L., and Olsen, M. G. (1975) Environmental differentiation and familiarity as determinants of children's memory for spatial location. *Developmental Psychology 11:* 495–501.

Aiken, E. G. (1971) Linguistic and imaginal mnemonics in paired-associate recall. *Psychonomic Science 24:* 91–93.

Alcorn, S. (1945) Development of the Tadoma method for the deaf-blind. *Journal of Exceptional Children 11:* 117–119.

Allport, D. A., Antonis, B., and Reynolds, P. (1972) On the division of attention: a disproof of the single channel hypothesis. *Quarterly Journal of Experimental Psychology 24:* 225–235.

Anderson, J. R., and Bower, G. H. (1973) *Human associative memory.* New York: V. H. Winston.

Antrobus, John S., Antrobus, Judith S., and Singer, J. L. (1964) Eye-movements accompanying daydreaming, visual imagery, and thought suppression. *Journal of Abnormal and Social Psychology 69:* 244–252.

Atkinson, R. C. (1975) Mnemotechnics in second-language learning. *American Psychologist 30:* 821–828.

Atwood, G. (1971) An experimental study of visual imagination and memory. *Cognitive Psychology 2:* 239–289.

Ball, F., Wood, C., and Smith, E. E. (1975) When are semantic targets detected faster than acoustic ones? *Perception and Psychophysics 17:* 1–8.

Bartlett, F. C. (1932) *Remembering.* Cambridge, England: Cambridge University Press.

Beller, H. K. (1971) Priming: Effects of advance information on matching. *Journal of Experimental Psychology 87:* 176–182.

Bever, T. G. and Terrace, H. S., eds. (1973) *Human behavior: Prediction and control in modern society.* Andover, Massachusetts: Warner Modular Publications.

Biederman, I. (1972) Perceiving real-world scenes. *Science 177:* 77–80.

Biederman, I., Glass, A. L., and Stacy, E. W. (1973) Searching for objects in real-world scenes. *Journal of Experimental Psychology 97:* 22–27.

Bobrow, D. G., and Norman, D. A. (In press) Some principles of memory schemata. In *Representation and Understanding.* (D. G. Bobrow and A. M. Collins, eds.) New York: Academic Press.

Bobrow, S. A., and Bower, G. H. (1969) Comprehension and recall of sentences. *Journal of Experimental Psychology 80:* 455–461.

Boulding, K. E. (1961) *The image.* Ann Arbor, Michigan: University of Michigan Press.

Bower, G. H. (1970) Analysis of a mnemonic device. *American Scientist* 496–510.

Bower, G. H. (1972) Mental imagery and Associative learning. In *Cognition in learning and memory.* (L. Gregg, ed.) New York: Wiley.

Bower, T. G. R. (1966) The visual world of infants. *Scientific American 215*(12): 80–92.

Bower, T. G. R. (1967) The development of object-permanence: Some studies of existence constancy. *Perception and Psychophysics 2:* 411–418.

Bower, T. G. R. (1971) The object in the world of the infant. *Scientific American 225* (4): 30–38.

Bower, T. G. R. (1974) *Development in infancy.* San Francisco: W. H. Freeman.

Bower, T. G. R., Broughton, J. M., and Moore, M. K. (1970a) Demonstration of intention in the reaching behavior of neonate humans. *Nature 228:* 679–681.

Bower, T. G. R., Broughton, J. M., and Moore, M. K. (1970b) The coordination of visual and tactual input in infants. *Perception and Psychophysics 8:* 51–53.

Bowers, K. S. (1976) Hypnotic dissociation and the dichotic listening paradigm. (Unpublished manuscript, Waterloo University.)

Brand, J. (1971) Classification without identification in visual search. *Quarterly Journal of Experimental Psychology 23:* 178–186.

Bransford, J. D., Barclay, J. R., and Franks, J. J. (1972) Sentence Memory—a constructive versus interpretive approach. *Cognitive Psychology 3:* 193–209.

Bransford, J. D., and Franks, J. J. (1971) The abstraction of linguistic ideas. *Cognitive Psychology 2:* 331–350.

Bransford, J. D., and Johnson, M. K. (1973) Consideration of some problems of comprehension. In *Visual information processing.* (W. G. Chase, ed.) New York: Academic Press.

Broadbent, D. E. (1958) *Perception and communication.* New York: Pergamon Press.

Broadbent, D. E. (1966) The well-ordered mind. *American Educational Research Journal 3:* 281–295.

Bronfenbrenner, U. (1974) Developmental research, public policy, and the ecology of childhood. *Child Development 45:* 1–5.

Brooks, L. R. (1967) The suppression of visualization in reading. *Quarterly Journal of Experimental Psychology 19:* 288–299.

Brooks, L. R. (1968) Spatial and verbal components of the act of recall. *Canadian Journal of Psychology 22:* 349–368.

Brown, A. L. (1975) The development of memory: knowing, knowing about knowing, and knowing how to know. In *Advances in child development and behavior 10.* (H. L. Reese, ed.) New York: Academic Press.

Brown, R. (1973) A *first language: the early stages*. Cambridge, Mass.: Harvard University Press.

Bruner, J. S. (1951) Personality dynamics and the process of perceiving. In *Perception—an approach to personality*. (R. R. Blake and G. V. Ramsey, eds.) New York: Ronald Press.

Bruner, J. S. (1957) Going beyond the information given. In J. S. Bruner et al., *Contemporary approaches to cognition: the Colorado symposium*. Cambridge, Mass.: Harvard University Press.

Bruner, J. S. (1973) *Beyond the information given: studies in the psychology of knowing*. New York: W. W. Norton.

Bruner, J. S. (1975) The ontogenesis of speech acts. *Journal of Child Language 2:* 1–19.

Brunswik, E. (1956) *Perception and the representative design of psychological experiments*. Berkeley: University of California Press.

Bryden, M. P. (1972) Perceptual strategies, attention, and memory. *University of Waterloo research reports in psychology* No. 43.

Byrne, B. (1974) Item concreteness vs. spatial organization as predictors of visual imagery. *Memory and Cognition 2:* 53–59.

Campbell, F. W., and Robson, J. G. (1968) Application of Fourier analysis to the visibility of gratings. *Journal of Physiology* (London) *197:* 551–556.

Chase, W. G., ed. (1973) *Visual information processing*. New York: Academic Press.

Chase, W. G., and Simon, H. A. (1973) The mind's eye in chess. In *Visual information processing*. (W. G. Chase, ed.) New York: Academic Press.

Cherry, E. C. (1953) Some experiments on the recognition of speech, with one and with two ears. *Journal of the Acoustical Society of America 25:* 975–979.

Cherry, E. C., and Taylor, W. K. (1954) Some further experiments on the recognition of speech with one and two ears. *Journal of the Acoustical Society of America 26:* 554–559.

Cohen, G. (1970) Search times for combinations of visual, phonemic, and semantic targets in reading prose. *Perception and Psychophysics 8:* 370–372.

Cole, M., Gay, J., Glick, J. A., and Sharp, D. W. (1971) *The cultural context of learning and thinking.* New York: Basic Books.

Cole, R. A., and Scott, B. (1974a) Toward a theory of speech perception. *Psychological Review 81:* 348–374.

Cole, R. A., and Scott, B. (1974b) The phantom in the phoneme: invariant cues for stop consonants. *Perception and Psychophysics 15:* 101–107.

Collyer, S. C., Jonides, J., and Bevan, W., (1972) Images as memory aids: is bizarreness helpful? *American Journal of Psychology 85:* 31–38.

Coltheart, M. (1972) Visual information-processing. In *New horizons in psychology 2.* (P. C. Dodwell, ed.) Harmondsworth, England: Penguin.

Cooper, L. A. (1975) Mental transformations of random two-dimensional shapes. *Cognitive Psychology 7:*20–43.

Cooper, L.A. (1976) Demonstration of a mental analog of an external rotation. *Perception and Psychophysics 19:* 296–302.

Cooper, L. A., and Podgorny, P. (1975) Mental transformations and visual comparison processes: effects of complexity and similarity. *Journal of Experimental Psychology: Human Perception and Performance.*

Cooper, L. A., and Shepard, R. N. (1973) Chronometric studies of the rotation of mental images. In *Visual Information Processing.* (W. G. Chase, Ed.) New York: Academic Press.

Corteen, R. S., and Dunn, D. (1974) Shock-associated words in a non-attended message: A test for momentary awareness. *Journal of Experimental Psychology 102:* 1134–1144.

Corteen, R. S., and Wood, B. (1972) Autonomic responses to shock-associated words in an unattended channel. *Journal of Experimental Psychology 94:* 308–313.

Craik, F. I. M., and Lockhart, R. S. (1972) Levels of processing: a framework for memory research. *Journal of Verbal Learning and Verbal Behavior* 11: 671–684.

Craik, F. I. M., and Tulving, E. (1975) Depth of processing and the retention of words in episodic memory. *Journal of Experimental Psychology: General, 104:* 268–294.

Descartes, R. (1638) *La dioptrique.* Leiden.

Deutsch, J. A., and Deutsch, D. (1963) Attention: Some theoretical considerations. *Psychological Review 70:* 80–90.

Deutsch, J. A., Deutsch, D., and Lindsay, P. H. (1967) Comments on "Selective attention: Perception or response?" *Quarterly Journal of Experimental Psychology 19:* 362–363.

Dirks, J., and Neisser, U. (In press) Memory for objects in real scenes: the development of recognition and recall. *Journal of Experimental Child Psychology.*

Doob, L. W. (1964) Eidetic images among the Ibo. *Ethnology 3:* 357–363.

Doob, L. W. (1965) Exploring eidetic imagery among the Kamba of central Kenya. *Journal of Social Psychology 67:* 3–22.

Doob, L. W. (1966) Eidetic imagery: a cross-cultural will-o'-the-wisp? *Journal of Psychology 63:* 13–34.

Doob, L. W. (1970) Correlates of eidetic imagery in Africa. *Journal of Psychology 76:* 223–230.

Dooling, D. J., and Lachman, R. (1971) Effects of comprehension on retention of prose. *Journal of Experimental Psychology 88:* 216–222.

Downey, J. E., and Anderson, J. E. (1915) Automatic writing. *American Journal of Psychology 26:* 161–195.

Downs, R. M., and Stea, D., eds. (1973) *Image and environment.* Chicago: Aldine Press.

Dreyfus, H. L. (1972) *What computers can't do.* New York: Harper & Row.

Dyer, F. N. (1973) The Stroop phenomenon and its use in the study of perceptual, cognitive, and response processes. *Memory and Cognition 1:* 106–120.

Eimas, P. D., Siqueland, E. P., Jusczyk, P., and Vigorito, J. (1971) Speech perception in infants. *Science 171:* 303–306.

Erdelyi, M. H. (1974) A new look at the new look: Perceptual defense and vigilance. *Psychological Review 81:* 1–25.

Erman, L. D. (1975) Overview of the HEARSAY speech understanding research. *Computer Science Research Review 1974-75.* Pittsburgh: Carnegie-Mellon University.

Feldman, M. (1968) Eidetic imagery in Ghana: a cross-cultural will-o'-the-wisp? *Journal of Psychology 69:* 259–269.

Flavell, J. H. (1970) Developmental studies of mediated memory. In *Advances in child development and behavior 5.* (H. W. Reese and L. P. Lipsitt, eds.) New York: Academic Press.

Fodor, J. A., Bever, T. G., and Garrett, M. F. (1974) *The psychology of language.* New York: McGraw-Hill.

Freud, S. (1900) *The Interpretation of Dreams.* Reprinted in *Basic writings of Sigmund Freud.* (A. A. Brill, ed.) New York: Modern Library, 1938.

Freud, S. (1905) *Three contributions to the theory of sex.* Reprinted in *Basic Writings of Sigmund Freud.* (A. A. Brill, ed.) New York: Modern Library, 1938.

Furst, B. (1948) *Stop forgetting.* Garden City, N.Y.: Garden City Books.

Garcia, J., Ervin, F. R., and Koelling, R. A. (1966) Learning with prolonged delay of reinforcement. *Psychonomic Science 5:* 121–122.

Garner, W. R. (1974) *The processing of information and structure.* Potomac, Md.: Lawrence Erlbaum Associates.

Gibson, E. J. (1969) *Principles of perceptual learning and development.* New York: Appleton-Century-Crofts.

Gibson, E. J. (In press) How perception really develops: a view from outside the system. In *Basic processes in reading: perception and comprehension.* (D. LaBerge and S. J. Samuels, eds.) Potomac, Md.: Lawrence Erlbuam Associates.

Gibson, E. J., and Levin, H. (1975) *The psychology of reading.* Cambridge, Mass.: MIT Press.

Gibson, J. J. (1950) *The perception of the visual world.* Boston: Houghton Mifflin.

Gibson, J. J. (1961) Ecological Optics. *Vision Research 1:* 253–262.

Gibson, J. J. (1962) Observations on active touch. *Psychological Review 69:* 477–491.

Gibson, J. J. (1966) *The senses considered as perceptual systems.* Boston: Houghton Mifflin.

Gibson, J. J. (1976) *An ecological approach to visual perception.* Manuscript in preparation (Cornell University).

Gibson, J. J., and Gibson, E. J. (1955) Perceptual learning: differentiation or enrichment? *Psychological Review 62:* 32–41.

Gladwin, T. (1970) *East is a big bird.* Cambridge, Mass.: Harvard University Press.

Glucksberg, S., and Cowen, G. N. (1970) Memory for non-attended auditory material. *Cognitive Psychology 1:* 149–156.

Goffman, E. (1974) *Frame analysis.* Cambridge, Mass.: Harvard University Press.

Gordon, F. R. and Yonas, A. (In press) Sensitivity to binocular depth information in infants. *Journal of Experimental Child Psychology.*

Gray, C. R., and Gummerman, K. (1975) The enigmatic eidetic image: a critical examination of methods, data, and theories. *Psychological Bulletin 82:* 383–407.

Greenwald, A. G. (1970) A double stimulation test of ideomotor theory with implications for selective attention. *Journal of Experimental Psychology 84:* 392–398.

Gregory, R. L. (1970) *The intelligent eye.* New York: McGraw-Hill.

Gregory, R. L. (1973) The confounded eye. In *Illusion in nature and art.* (R. L. Gregory and E. H. Gombrich, eds.) London: Duckworth.

Gummerman, K., and Gray, C. R. (1971) Recall of visually-presented material: an unwonted case and a bibliography for eidetic imagery. *Psychonomic Monograph Supplements 4* (10, Whole No. 58).

Gunderson, K. (1971) *Mentality and machines.* Garden City, N.Y.: Doubleday Anchor.

Guzman, A. (1968) *Computer recognition of three-dimensional objects in a visual scene.* Cambridge, Mass.: MIT Project MAC, MAC-TR-59.

Haber, R. N. (1966) The nature of the effect of set on perception. *Psychological Review* 73: 335–350.

Haber, R. N., and Haber, R. B. (1964) Eidetic imagery: I. Frequency. *Perceptual and motor skills 19:* 131–138.

Hagen, J. W. (1967) The effect of distraction on selective attention. *Child Development 38:* 685–694.

Halle, M., and Stevens, K. S. (1964) Speech recognition: a model and a program for research. In *The structure of language: readings in the psychology of language.* (J. A. Foder and J. J. Katz, eds.) Englewood Cliffs, N.J.: Prentice-Hall.

Harris, C. S. (1965) Perceptual adaptation to inverted, reversed, and displaced vision. *Psychological Review 72:* 419–444.

Harris, P. L. (1975) Development of search and object permanence during infancy. *Psychological Bulletin 82:* 332–344.

Hawkins, R. P. (1973) Learning of peripheral content in films: a developmental study. *Child Development 44:* 214–217.

Hernandez-Peon, R. H., Scherrer, H., and Jouvet, M. (1956) Modification of electrical activity in the cochlear nucleus during attention in unanesthetized cats. *Science 123:* 331–332.

Hillyard, S. A., and Picton, T. W. (In press) Event-related brain potentials and selective information processing in man. In *The cerebral evoked potential in man.* (J. Desmedt, ed.) Oxford, England: Oxford University Press.

Hochberg, J. (1970) Attention, organization, and consciousness. In *Attention: contemporary theory and analysis.* (D. J. Mostovsky, ed.) New York: Appleton-Century-Crofts.

Hochberg, J. (1975) Motion pictures, eye movements, and mental maps: perception as purposive behavior. Address presented at the American Psychological Association, Chicago.

Hochberg, J., and Gellman, L. (1976) The effect of landmark features on "mental rotation" times. Unpublished manuscript (Columbia University).

Hockett, C. D. (1960) The origin of speech. *Scientific American* 203(9): 88–96.

Horowitz, M. J. (1970) *Image formation and cognition*. New York: Appleton-Century-Crofts.

Huttenlocher, J. (1974) The origins of language comprehension. In *Theories in cognitive psychology: the Loyola symposium*. (R. L. Solso, ed.) Potomac, Md.: Lawrence Erlbaum Associates.

Ingling, N. W. (1972) Categorization: a mechanism for rapid information processing. *Journal of Experimental Psychology* 94: 239–243.

Jack, C. E., and Thurlow, W. R. (1973) Effects of degree of visual association and angle of displacement on the "ventriloquism effect." *Perceptual and Motor Skills* 37: 967–979.

Janssen, W. H. (In press) Selective interference in paired associate and free recall learning: messing up the image. *Acta Psychologica*.

Jenkins, J. J. (1974) Remember that old theory of memory? Well, forget it! *American Psychologist* 29: 785–795.

Jensen, A. R., and Rohwer, W. D. (1966) The Stroop color-word test: a review. *Acta Psychologica* 25: 36–93.

Johansson, G. (1973) Visual perception of biological motion and a model for its analysis. *Perception and psychophysics* 14: 201–211.

Johnston, I. R., White, G. R., and Cumming, R. W. (1973) The role of optical expansion patterns in locomotor control. *American Journal of Psychology* 86: 311–324.

Johnston, J. C., and McClelland, J. L. (1974) Perception of letters in words: seek not and ye shall find. *Science 184:* 1192–1193.

Jonides, J., and Gleitman, H. (1972) A conceptual category effect in visual search: O as letter or as digit. *Perception and Psychophysics* 12: 457–460.

Jonides, J., Kahn, R., and Rozin, P. (1975) Imagery instructions improve memory in blind subjects. *Bulletin of the Psychonomic Society 5:* 424–426.

Just, M. A., and Carpenter, P. A. (In press) Eye fixations and cognitive processes. *Cognitive Psychology.*

Kagan, J. (1971) *Change and continuity in infancy.* New York: Wiley.

Kahneman, D. (1968) Method, findings, and theory in studies of visual masking. *Psychological Bulletin 70:* 404–425.

Kahneman, D. (1973) *Attention and effort.* Englewood Cliffs, N.J.: Prentice-Hall.

Kaplan, G. (1969) Kinetic disruption of optical texture: the perception of depth at an edge. *Perception and Psychophysics 6:* 193–198.

Klapp, S. T., and Lee, P. (1974) Time of occurrence cues for "unattended" auditory material. *Journal of Experimental Psychology 102:* 176–177.

Klatzky, R. (1975) *Human memory.* San Francisco: W. H. Freeman.

Kolers, P. A. (1968) Some psychological aspects of pattern recognition. In *Recognizing patterns.* (P. A. Kolers and M. Eden, Eds.) Cambridge, Mass.: MIT Press.

Kolers, P. A. (1969) Voluntary attention switching between foresight and hindsight. *Quarterly Progress Reports: Research Laboratory of Electronics, M.I.T.* No. 92: 381–385.

Kolers, P. A. (1972) *Aspects of motion perception.* New York: Pergamon Press.

Kosslyn, S. M. (1975) Information representation in visual images. *Cognitive Psychology 7:* 341–370.

Kosslyn, S. M., Pick, H. L., and Fariello, G. R. (1974) Cognitive maps in children and men. *Child Development 45:* 707–716.

Koulack, D. (1972) Rapid eye movements and visual imagery during sleep. *Psychological Bulletin 78:* 155–158.

Kreutzer, M. A., Leonard, C., and Flavell, J. H. (1975) An interview study of children's knowledge about memory.

Monographs of the Society for Research in Child Development Serial No. 159.

Kuhl, P. K. and Miller, J. D. (1975) Speech perception by the chinchilla: voiced-voiceless distinction in alveolar plosive consonants. *Science 190:* 69–72.

Lackner, J. R., and Garrett, M. F. (1972) Resolving ambiguity: effects of biasing context in the unattended ear. *Cognition 1:* 359–372.

Leask, J., Haber, R. N., and Haber, R. B. (1969) Eidetic imagery in children: II. Longitudinal and experimental results. *Psychonomic Monograph Supplements 3* (whole No. 35).

Lee, D. N., and Aronson, E. (1974) Visual proprioceptive control of standing in human infants. *Perception and Psychophysics 15:* 529–532.

Lefton, L. A. (1973) Metacontrast: a review. *Perception and Psychophysics 13:* 161–171.

Lewis, J. L. (1970) Semantic processing of unattended messages using dichotic listening, *Journal of Experimental Psychology 85:* 225–228.

Liberman, A. M. (1957) Some results of research on speech perception. *Journal of the Acoustical Society of America 24:* 590–594.

Liberman, A. M., Cooper, F. S., Shankweiler, D. P., and Studdert-Kennedy, M. (1967) Perception of the speech code. *Psychological Review 74:* 431–461.

Lindsay, P. N., and Norman, D. A. (1972) *Human information processing.* New York: Academic Press.

Lishman, J. R., and Lee, D. N. (1973) The autonomy of visual kinaesthesis. *Perception 2:* 287–294.

Littman, D., and Becklen, R. (In Press) Selective looking with minimal eye movements. *Perception and Psychophysics.*

Loftus, E. F. (1975) Leading questions and the eyewitness report. *Cognitive Psychology 7:* 560–572.

Loftus, E. F., and Palmer, J. C. (1974) Reconstruction of automobile destruction: An example of the interaction between language and memory. *Journal of Verbal Learning and Verbal Behavior* 11: 585–589.

Lorayne, H., & Lucas, J. (1974) *The memory book.* New York: Ballantine Books.

Luria, A. R. (1968) *The mind of a mnemonist.* New York: Basic Books.

Luria, A. R. (1975) Scientific perspectives and philosophical dead ends in modern linguistics. *Cognition 3:* 377–385.

Lykken, D. T. (1974) Psychology and the Lie Detector Industry. *American Psychologist 29:* 725–739.

Lynch, K. (1960) *The image of the city.* Cambridge, Mass.: MIT Press.

Lynch, K. (1972) *What time is this place?* Cambridge, Mass.: MIT Press.

Maas, J. B., and Johansson, G. (1972) *Motion perception: two-dimensional motion perception.* (Film and film guide.) Boston: Houghton Mifflin.

Maccoby, E. E., and Hagen, J. W. (1965) Effects of distraction upon central vs. incidental recall. *Journal of Experimental Child Psychology, 2:* 280–289.

Mackay, D. G. (1973) Aspects of the theory of comprehension, memory, and attention. *Quarterly Journal of Experimental Psychology 25:* 22–40.

Mackworth, N. H., and Bruner, J. S. (1970) How adults and children search and recognize pictures. *Human Development 13* (3): 149–177.

MacNamara, J. (1972) Cognitive basis of language learning in infants. *Psychological Review 79:* 1–13.

Mandel, I., and Bridger, W. H. (1973) Is there classical conditioning without cognitive expectancy? *Psychophysiology 10:* 87–90.

Mandler, J. M., and Parker, R. E. (1976) Memory for descriptive and spatial information in complex pictures. *Journal of Experimental Psychology: Human Learning and Memory 2:* 38–48.

Mandler, J. M., and Stein, N. L. (1974) Recall and recognition of pictures by children as a function of organization and distractor similarity. *Journal of Experimental Psychology 102:* 657–669.

Massaro, D. W. (1975) *Experimental psychology and information processing.* Chicago: Rand, McNally.

Menzel, E. W. (1973) Chimpanzee spatial memory organization. *Science 182:* 943–945.

Metzler, J., and Shepard, R. N. (1974) Transformational studies of the internal representation of three-dimensional objects. In *Theories of cognitive psychology: the Loyola symposium.* (R. L. Solso, ed.) Potomac, Md.: Lawrence Erlbaum Associates.

Miller, G. A., Galanter, E., and Pribram, K. H. (1960) *Plans and the structure of behavior.* New York: Holt, Rinehart, & Winston.

Miller, G. A., Heise, G. A., and Lichten, W. (1951) The intelligibility of speech as a function of the context of the test material. *Journal of Experimental Psychology 41:* 329–335.

Minsky, M. (1975) A framework for representing knowledge. In *The Psychology of Computer Vision.* (P. H. Winston, ed.) New York: McGraw-Hill.

Moray, N. (1959) Attention in dichotic listening: affective cues and the influence of instructions. *Quarterly Journal of Experimental Psychology, 11:* 56–60.

Moray, N. (1970) *Attention: selective processes in vision and hearing.* New York: Academic Press.

Morton, J. (1969) Interaction of information in word recognition. *Psychological Review 76:* 165–178.

Nakayama, K. and Loomis, J. M. (1974) Optical velocity patterns, velocity-sensitive neurons, and space perception: a hypothesis. *Perception 3:* 63–80.

Nappe, G. N., and Wollen, K. A. (1973) Effects of instructions to form common and bizarre mental images on retention. *Journal of Experimental Psychology 100:* 6–8.

Neisser, U. (1963) The imitation of man by machine. *Science 139:* 193–197.

Neisser, U. (1967) *Cognitive psychology.* New York: Appleton-Century-Crofts.

Neisser, U. (1972) Changing conceptions of imagery. In *The function and nature of imagery*. (P. N. Sheehan, ed.) New York: Academic Press.

Neisser, U. (1974) Practiced card-sorting for multiple targets. *Memory and cognition 2:* 781–785.

Neisser, U. (1975) Self-knowledge and psychological knowledge: Teaching psychology from the cognitive point of view. *The educational psychologist 11:* 158–170.

Neisser, U. (1976) General, academic, and artificial intelligence. In *The nature of intelligence.* (L. B. Resnick, ed). Hillsdale, N.J.: Lawrence Erlbaum Associates.

Neisser, U. (In press) Gibson's ecological optics: Consequences of a different stimulus description. *Journal of the Theory of Social Behavior.*

Neisser, U., and Becklen, R. (1975) Selective looking: attending to visually-specified events. *Cognitive Psychology 7:* 480–494.

Neisser, U., and Hupcey, J. (1975) A Sherlockian experiment. *Cognition 3:* 307–311.

Neisser, U., and Kerr, N. (1973) Spatial and mnemonic properties of visual images. *Cognitive Psychology 5:* 138–150.

Neisser, U., Novick, R., and Lazar, R. (1963) Searching for ten targets simultaneously. *Perceptual and Motor Skills 17:* 955–961.

Nelson, K. (1974) Concept, word, and sentence: interrelations in acquisition and development. *Psychological Review 81:* 267–285.

Newell, A. (1973) You can't play 20 questions with nature and win: projective comments on the papers of this symposium. In *Visual information processing.* (W. G. Chase, ed.) New York: Academic Press.

Newell, A., Shaw, J. C., and Simon, H. A. (1958) Elements of a theory of human problem solving. *Psychological Review 65:* 151–166.

Newell, A., and Simon, H. A. (1972) *Human problem solving.* Englewood Cliffs, N. J.: Prentice-Hall.

Newtson, D. (In press) Foundations of Attribution: the perception of ongoing behavior. In *New Directions in attribu-*

tion research. (J. Harvey, N. Ickes, and R. Kidd, eds.) Potomac, Md.: Lawrence Erlbaum Associates.

Orne, M. T. (1962) On the social psychology of the psychological experiment: With particular reference to demand characteristics and their implications. *American Psychologist 17:* 776–783.

Paivio, A. (1971) *Imagery and verbal processes.* New York: Holt, Rhinehart, & Winston.

Paris, S. G., and Carter, A. Y. (1973) Semantic and constructive aspects of sentence memory in children. *Developmental Psychology 9:* 109–113.

Perky, C. W. (1910) An experimental study of imagination. *American Journal of Psychology 21:* 422–452.

Piaget, J. (1952) *The origins of intelligence in children.* New York: International Universities Press.

Piaget, J. (1954) *The construction of reality in the child.* New York: Basic Books.

Pick, H. L. (1972) Mapping children—mapping space. Paper presented at the American Psychological Association, Honolulu.

Picton, T. A., Hillyard, S. A., Galambos, R., and Schiff, M. (1971) Human auditory attention: a central or peripheral process? *Science 171:* 351–353.

Pillsbury, W. B. (1897) A study in apperception. *American Journal of Psychology 8:* 315–393.

Posner, M. I. (1973a) Coordination of internal codes. In *Visual information processing.* (W. G. Chase, ed.) New York: Academic Press.

Posner, M. I. (1973b) *Cognition: an introduction.* Glenview, Illinois: Scott, Foresman.

Posner, M. I., Boies, S. J., Eichelman, W. H., and Taylor, R. L. (1969) Retention of visual and name codes of single letters. *Journal of Experimental Psychology Monographs 79,* No. 3: Part 2, 1–16.

Posner, M. I., and Mitchell, R. F. (1967) Chronometric analysis of classification. *Psychological Review 74:* 392–409.

Posner, M. ., and Snyder, C. R. R. (1975) Attention and cognitive control. In *Information processing and cognition: the Loyola symposium.* (R. Solso, ed.) Potomac, Md.: Lawrence Erlbaum Associates.

Potter, M. C. (1975) Meaning in visual search. *Science 187:* 965–966.

Price-Williams, D. R., Gordon, W., and Ramirez, W. (1969) Skill and conservation: A study of pottery-making children. *Developmental Psychology 1:* 769.

Pritchatt, D. (1968) An investigation in some of the underlying associative verbal processes of the Stroop color-word task. *Quarterly Journal of Experimental Psychology 20:* 351–359.

Pylyshyn, Z. W. (1973) What the mind's eye tells the mind's brain: A critique of mental imagery. *Psychological Bulletin 80:* 1–24.

Reed, S. K. (1973) *Psychological process in pattern recognition.* New York: Academic Press.

Richardson, A. (1969) *Mental imagery.* New York: Springer.

Rock, I., and Harris, C. S. (1967) Vision and touch. *Scientific American 216* (5): 96–104.

Rosch, E. (1973) Natural categories. *Cognitive Psychology 4:* 328–350.

Rosch, E. (1975) Cognitive representations of semantic categories. *Journal of Experimental Psychology: General 104:* 192–233.

Rosch, E. (In press.) Universals and cultural specifics in human categorization. In *Cross-cultural perspectives on learning.* (R. Brislin, S. Bochern, and W. Lonner, eds.) New York: Sage/Halsted.

Rosenthal, R. (1966) *Experimenter effects in behavioral research.* New York: Appleton-Century-Crofts.

Ross, J., and Lawrence, K. A. (1968) Some observations on memory artifice. *Psychonomic Science 13:* 107–108.

Rumelhart, D. E. (In press (1975)) Notes on a schema for stories. In *Representation and understanding* (D. G. Bobrow and A. M. Collins, eds.). New York: Academic Press.

Rumelhart, D. E. (In press) Understanding and summarizing brief stories. In *Basic processes in reading: perception and comprehension* (D. LaBerge and J. Samuels, eds.) Hillsdale, N.J.: Lawrence Erlbaum Associates.

Rumelhart, D. E. and Ortony, A. (In press) The representation of knowledge in memory. In *Schooling and the acquisition of knowledge.* (R. C. Anderson, R. J. Spiro, and W. E. Montague, eds.) Hillsdale, N.J.: Lawrence Erlbaum Associates.

Sachs, J. S. (1967) Recognition memory for syntactic and semantic aspects of connected discourse. *Perception and Psychophysics 2:* 437–442.

Sachs, J. S. (1974) Memory in reading and listening to discourse. *Memory and Cognition 2:* 95–100.

Sakitt, B. (1975) Locus of short-term visual storage. *Science 190:* 1318–1319.

Salthouse, T. (1974) Using selective interference to investigate spatial memory representation. *Memory and Cognition 2:* 749–757.

Salthouse, T. (1975) Simultaneous processing of verbal and spatial information. *Memory and Cognition 3:* 221–225.

Scarborough, D. L. (1972) Memory for brief visual displays of symbols. *Cognitive Psychology,* 1972, *3:* 408–429.

Schachtel, E. G. (1947) On memory and childhood amnesia. *Psychiatry 10:* 1–26.

Scribner, S. (1974) Developmental aspects of categorized recall in a West African society. *Cognitive Psychology 6:* 475–494.

Scribner, S., and Cole, M. (1973) Cognitive consequences of formal and informal education. *Science 182:* 553–559.

Segal, S. J. (1971a) Processing of the stimulus in imagery and perception. In *Imagery: current cognitive approaches.* (S. J. Segal, ed.) New York: Academic Press.

Segal, S. J., ed. (1971b) *Imagery: Current Cognitive Approaches.* New York: Academic Press.

Segal, S. J. (1972) Assimilation of a stimulus in the construction of an image: the Perky effect revisited. In *The function and nature of imagery.* (P. W. Sheehan, ed.) New York: Academic Press.

Segal, S. J., and Fusella, V. (1970) Influence of imaged pictures and sounds on detection of visual and auditory signals. *Journal of Experimental Psychology 83:* 458–464.

Sekuler, R. (1974) Spatial vision. *Annual Review of Psychology 25:* 195–232.

Selfridge, O. G. (1959) Pandemonium: a paradigm for learning. In *The mechanisation of thought processes.* London: H. M. Stationery Office.

Seligman, M. E. P., and Hager, J. L., eds. (1972) *Biological boundaries of learning.* New York: Appleton-Century-Crofts.

Shaffer, L. H. (1975) Multiple attention in continuous verbal tasks. In *Attention and performance V.* (P. M. A. Rabbitt and S. Dornic, eds.) New York: Academic Press.

Shannon, C. E. (1948) A mathematical theory of communication. *Bell System Technical Journal 27:* 379–423, 623–656.

Sheehan, P. W., ed. (1972) *The function and nature of imagery.* New York: Academic Press.

Sheehan, P. W., and Neisser, U. (1969) Some variables affecting the vividness of imagery in recall. *British Journal of Psychology 60:* 71–80.

Shepard, R. N., and Metzler, J. (1971) Mental rotation of three-dimensional objects. *Science 171:* 701–703.

Sherif, M. (1935) A study of some social factors in perception. *Archives of Psychology* No. 187.

Shiffrin, R. M. (In press) Capacity limitations in information processing, attention, and memory. In *Handbook of learning and cognitive processes: volume 4, attention and memory.* (W. K. Estes, ed.) Hillsdale, N.J.: Lawrence Erlbaum Associates.

Shiffrin, R. M., and Gardner, G. T. (1972) Visual processing capacity and attentional control. *Journal of Experimental Psychology 93:* 72–82.

Shiffrin, R. M., and Grantham, D. W. (1974) Can attention be allocated to sensory modalities? *Perception and Psychophysics 15:* 460–474.

Shiffrin, R. M., Pisoni, D. B., and Castaneda-Mendez, K. (1974) Is attention shared between the ears? *Cognitive Psychology 6:* 190–215.

Siegel, A. W., and Stevenson, H. W. (1966) Incidental learning: A developmental study. *Child Development 37:* 811–817.

Siegel, A. W., and White, S. H. (1975) The development of spatial representation of large-scale environments. In *Advances in child development and behavior 10.* (H. W. Reese, ed.) New York: Academic Press.

Simon, H. A., and Barenfeld, M. (1969) Information processing analysis of perceptual processes in problem solving. *Psychological Review 76:* 473–483.

Simon, H. A., and Chase, W. G. (1973) Skill in chess. *American Scientist 61:* 394–403.

Skinner, B. F. (1971) *Beyond freedom and dignity.* New York: Knopf.

Solomons, L., and Stein, G. (1896) Normal motor automatism. *Psychological Review 3:* 492–512.

Spelke, E. (1976) Infants' intermodal perception of events. *Cognitive Psychology 8:* 553–560.

Spelke, E., Hirst, W., and Neisser, U. (1976) Skills of divided attention. *Cognition 4:* 215–230.

Sperling, G. (1960) The information available in brief visual presentations. *Psychological Monographs 74:* No. 11.

Sternberg, S. (1966) High-speed scanning in human memory. *Science 153:* 652–654.

Sternberg, S. (1975) Memory scanning: New findings and current controversies. *Quarterly Journal of Experimental Psychology 27:* 1–32.

Stromeyer, C. F. III (1970) Eidetikers. *Psychology Today* (Nov.), 76–80.

Stromeyer, C. F. III, and Psotka, J. (1970) The detailed texture of eidetic images. *Nature 225:* 346–349.

Stroop, J. R. (1935) Studies of interference in serial verbal reaction. *Journal of Experimental Psychology 18:* 643–662.

Sumby, W. H., and Pollack, I. (1954) Visual contribution to speech intelligibility in noise. *Journal of the Acoustical Society of America 26:* 212–215.

Thurlow, W. R., and Jack, C. E. (1973) Certain determinants of the "ventriloquism effect." *Perceptual and Motor Skills 36:* 1171–1184.

Tolman, E. C. (1948) Cognitive maps in rats and men. *Psychological Review 55:* 189–208.

Treisman, A. M. (1960) Contextual cues in selective listening. *Quarterly Journal of Experimental Psychology 12:* 242–248.

Treisman, A. M. (1964a) Monitoring and storage of irrelevant messages in selective attention. *Journal of Verbal Learning and Verbal Behavior 3:* 449–459.

Treisman, A. M. (1964b) Selective attention in man. *British Medical Bulletin 20:* 12–16.

Treisman, A. M. (1969) Strategies and models of selective attention. *Psychological Review 76:* 282–299.

Treisman, A. M., and Geffen, G. (1967) Selective attention: Perception or response? *Quarterly Journal of Experimental Psychology 19:* 1–17, 365–367.

Treisman, A. M., and Riley, J. G. R. (1969) Is selective attention selective perception or selective response? A further test. *Journal of Experimental Psychology 79:* 27–34.

Treisman, A. M., Squire, R., and Green, J. (1974) Semantic processes in selective listening? A replication. *Memory and Cognition 2:* 641–646.

Tulving, E., and Thomson, D. M. (1973) Encoding specificity and retrieval processes in episodic memory. *Psychological Review 80:* 352–373.

Turnbull, C. M. (1961) *The forest people: a study of the Pygmies of the Congo.* New York: Simon & Schuster.

Turvey, M. T. (1973) On peripheral and central processes in vision: Inference from an information-processing analysis of masking with patterned stimuli. *Psychological Review 80:* 1–52.

Underwood, G. (1974) Moray vs. the rest: the effects of extended shadowing practice. *Quarterly Journal of Experimental Psychology 26:* 368–372.

von Wright, J. M., Anderson, K., and Stenman, U. (1975) Generalization of conditioned GSRs in dichotic listening. In *Attention and performance V.* (P. M. A. Rabbitt and S. Dornic, eds.) New York: Academic Press.

Vygotsky, L. S. (1962) *Thought & language.* Cambridge, Mass.: MIT Press.

Wallach, H., and O'Connell, D. N. (1953) The kinetic depth effect. *Journal of Experimental Psychology 45:* 205–207.

Waltz, D. (1975) Understanding line drawings of scenes with shadows. In *The Psychology of Computer Vision.* (P. H. Winston, ed.) New York: McGraw-Hill.

Wardlaw, K. A., and Kroll, N. E. A. (In press) Autonomic responses to shock-associated words in a non-attended message: a failure to replicate. *Journal of Experimental Psychology: Human Perception and Performance.*

Waters, R. S., and Wilson, W. A., Jr. (1976) Speech perception in rhesus monkeys; the voicing distinction between synthesized labial and velar stop consonants. *Perception and psychophysics 19:* 285–289.

Warren, R. (In press) The perception of egomotion. *Journal of experimental psychology: human perception and performance.*

Weisstein, N., and Harris, C. S. (1974) Visual detection of line segments: an object-superiority effect. *Science 186:* 752–755.

Wertheimer, M. (1961) Psychomotor coordination of auditory and visual space at birth. *Science 134:* 1962.

Wheeler, D. D. (1970) Processes in word recognition. *Cognitive Psychology 1:* 59–85.

Wilson, E. O. (1975) *Sociobiology.* Cambridge, Mass.: Harvard University Press.

Winograd, T. (1972). Understanding natural language. *Cognitive Psychology 3:* 1–191.

Winston, P. H., ed. (1975) *The psychology of computer vision.* New York: McGraw-Hill.

Wolff, P. H., and White, B. L. (1965) Visual pursuit and attention in young infants. *Journal of the American Academy of Child Psychiatry 4:* 473–484.

Wollen, K. A., Weber, A., and Lowry, D. H. (1972) Bizarreness versus interaction of mental images as determinants of learning. *Cognitive Psychology 3:* 518–523.

Woodworth, R. S. (1938) *Experimental psychology.* New York: Holt.

Worden, F. G. (1966) Attention and auditory electrophysiology. In *Progress in physiological psychology, volume I.* (E. Stellar and J. M. Sprague, eds.) New York: Academic Press.

Yates, F. A. (1966) *The art of memory.* London: Routledge & Kegan Paul.

Yonas, A., and Pittenger, J. (1973) Searching for many targets: an analysis of speed & accuracy. *Perception and Psychophysics 13:* 513–516.

Name Index

Subject Index